HOW TO PAINT FOR PLEASURE

BOWL OF ANEMONES: R. O. DUNLOP, R.A.

A simple arrangement in oil with palette knife; and a
satisfying ensemble.

How to
PAINT
For Pleasure

A HANDBOOK FOR BEGINNERS

R. O. Dunlop, R.A.

PELLEGRINI & CUDAHY
NEW YORK

Library of Congress Catalogue Card Number: 51-12759

Copyright, 1952, by R. O. Dunlop

Published simultaneously in Canada
by George J. McLeod, Ltd., Toronto.
Manufactured in the United States of America
by H. Wolff Book Manufacturing Company,
New York.

CONTENTS

But (adds the publisher) there is a great deal in this book which cannot be listed here: all the rich experience that a painter of many years' practice can give without stint to the doubtful beginner: ranging from such details as the kind of pencil to use and the brushes you should buy to philosophical advice on the best approach to painting or drawing if you are *to please yourself*—that's what matters.

COLOR PLATES

ILLUSTRATIONS

And twenty line drawings throughout the text

HOW TO PAINT FOR PLEASURE

1. Why Paint?
Or the Pictorial View of Life

I WOULD love to paint but I can't draw a straight line! How often has one heard that. The fact that there is the wish to paint is the thing that matters. Painting is not difficult if one just drops the self-consciousness that makes one feel incompetent. Take courage and make a start. Try not to be too self-critical, too anxious to do wonders, too proud, to be just a beginner. Even the greatest masters of painting were never satisfied, for the amount to learn is always more than the amount learned.

To practice painting or sketching is undoubtedly soothing to the nerves, for you are usually out in the open air in front of nature, and the smallness and petty foibles of your daily life are forgotten. In these difficult days it is more than ever a benefit to practice an art that takes you outside yourself and gives refreshment to your inner self, which so needs sustenance.

There are those who visit the great art galleries, such as the Metropolitan Museum in New York, the Chicago Art Institute, the National Gallery in Washington, or the famous galleries in cities such as San Francisco, Minneapolis, Cincinnati, Boston, and Philadelphia, and who come away with the feeling that they also would like to draw and paint—to produce works of art. That is one important function of all these great exhibitions of pictures in the national collections and in the small local exhibitions: to show those who have eyes to see what beauty they can behold and how to attempt a creative response to beauty in their own lives. They open the eyes and encourage a desire to paint. It has been said that all good paintings create new painters, that there is a creative germ living in the picture which by some means or other becomes injected into the life stream of the beholder and makes him or her long to go and do likewise. It is really only the sad lack of courage, of self-confidence, that stops most of these aspirants from going out and getting brushes and paints and starting straightaway to portray their own particular view and vision of the things they see.

There are many who wish to have a greater understanding of the details of nature's wonder but who do not realize that by sketching and painting out of doors they will come by this real knowledge in a most interesting way. Facts are easy to gather, but an intimate understanding is come by only with close and attentive observation—and that is most easily accomplished when one is painting out of doors, quietly poised before nature, and in a receptive mood.

There are those who love color, all sorts of color, from bright orange, red, and scarlet to deep green and blue and purple. For these people, to paint is to express their mood about color, to transfer their emotional response to paper or canvas, to add one color to another or by the side of another, in order to make a joyous pattern.

One of the greatest art teachers I knew always gave encouragement and never adverse criticism when looking at a beginner's work. It is by receiving encouragement that the artist in you grows. Just suppose you had never drawn a teapot before and you make a brave effort, putting down on paper the curve of the spout and the corresponding curve of the handle; then you fill in the round bowl and then—alas—you make a mess of the lid and the base—what does it matter? The essentials of what you have seen are there and you will find that there is life and vitality in your sketch, rather than accuracy of detail. It is the gift of the art teacher to inspire the *vision* and not to criticize the lack of *imitative ability.* Any photograph can give the precise details of a teapot, but see Figure 1.

There is no intention in these pages to help you to increase your income or make a second business string to your bow. In fact, although the amateur painter may occasionally be lucky and sell one of his efforts, he would do well to regard his drawing and painting entirely as a form of self-expression and not expect financial reward. Such a rule gives a freedom from ties of any sort. The fact of working for a given audience or

FIGURE 1. *Catching the essentials of an ornamental teapot.*

with the hope of selling what you create, is invariably a deterrent to your real self-expression.

There is no doubt that you attain a more enlightened view of the work of the old and modern masters of painting that you see in galleries and exhibitions after having tried your own hand at drawing and painting. There is nothing like a little practical knowledge to awaken sympathy with, and understanding of, works of art. Many critics of modern art would not have written half the nonsense they have put into print, had they themselves had some practical experience in painting. Those who love looking at paintings should see to it that they try their hand at producing something themselves.

THE PICTORIAL VIEW OF LIFE

Life can be seen from many aspects. There is the ordinary common-or-garden view, where everything has its purpose: an egg is to eat, a house is to live in, a street is to walk down, a bus is to travel on, and so on—this is the utilitarian view; and for most of us, for most of the time, this is the only view we take.

There is the musician's view in which life becomes *sound* and all things are a series of related sounds and chords. There is the poet's view in which life is a series of ideas, concepts, images, forming themselves into words that have rhythm and sequence.

And there is the painter's view in which the world is a series of shapes, colors, lines, related into ever-changing visual patterns. Those who desire to paint what they see around them have to acquire the habit of seeing life in this pictorial way. They have to dismiss from their minds, temporarily, the matter-of-fact, day-to-day view and to begin instead to visualize in terms

7

of shape, in terms of line, in terms of color. This, maybe, is the first hurdle to jump, for those who wish to paint *life*. It is not always easy to see things apart from their practical use, to see things in a fresh pictorial way, but that is what must be done from the outset, and once the new outlook is acquired it will open up unlimited possibilities for new visual impressions of even the most stale and familiar things. Life will be renewed.

SEEING AND LOOKING

It is easy to look but not so easy to *see*. When you begin to take an interest in the shape of things—the outline of a vase, or the actual formation of a face, eyebrows related to nose, nose to chin, cheekbones to forehead—then you realize that for the most part you do not *see* at all, but just take in vague impressions, relating nothing to its surroundings, and having only the foggiest notion of shape, color, or line.

It is wise, when beginning to search for shape and color, to start with some easy thing that you can see often and yet might usually overlook. Let us take a table set for tea, or perhaps one that has just been left after tea is finished. Let us sit and look at the table quietly and with affection for everything on it, from cloth to breadboard. Let us see the outstanding things first, the large teapot, the milk jug, the loaf of bread—

then the cups and saucers, the plates, the knives, the jam pot and butter dish. Let us find the shapes of these things in simple outline and relate them one to another. Once you have discovered the shape in your mind's eye it is easy to draw its outline, so now take a pencil and define a space on a piece of paper, an oblong say 5 inches by 3 inches, and draw in the outline of the chief objects as they are related one to the other. Then look again for the tone and color arrangement of these things, light or dark, white or blue, and see how in the merest chance setting of a tea table you can find order and pattern. A design begins to emerge where before one saw only a jumble of used crockery and the untidy remains of a meal. I have illustrated this in Figure 2.

The casual arrangement is always better than a grouping which has been carefully planned. If you look long enough and deeply enough at the most seemingly jumbled array of objects, gradually you will begin to see design and order in the chaos. If you start rearranging things to put them in what you *think* is a better order they will, in nine cases out of ten, become much stiffer and more stilted and will lose natural design.

Keep on looking closely at things wherever you are, in bus, train, street, at a baseball game or a dance. See the relationships of shapes and colors, how reds will grow up with reds or blues with blues, with a splash of black or white to serve as foil. It is a good idea to half-close one's eyes when searching out the *masses* of things so that the *details* do not obtrude. Especially is this true of looking at landscape. Try deliberately to see the large mass-shape of trees against the sky, not the details of the foliage.

FIGURE 2. *Table after luncheon.*

Always bear in mind that the space of the canvas or paper or board, or the page in the sketch book, is your world inside which you are creating your design, your picture. You are not, of necessity, copying the things before you; you are using the shapes and lines they suggest to you and re-creating them to fit in with your own feelings, your emotions, your thoughts: remembering of course that nature, in all its multiplicity, is your never-failing guide at all times, everywhere.

It is as well to be simple, receptive, and modest in front of nature rather than bombastic or too self-assertive, but on the other hand it does not do to be nervous or hesitant. Courage is certainly necessary; a stout heart, a willingness to take risks and never mind spoiling paper or canvas or wasting paint. If you think a color is pink, make it pink, and never mind what anyone else would say. Always be definite rather than vague about your shapes and colors.

THE IMPERSONAL ATTITUDE

Perhaps it would be as well to enlarge upon this question of the attitude of the artist to his work. It is the acquisition of this attitude which is of such great benefit to those who begin to draw and paint for their own pleasure.

Detachment from one's little day-to-day anxieties—from intense personal preoccupation with, and worry over, things—is good for everyone. To observe things instead of glancing at them, to note exact shapes, particular colors, the light and shade on objects, means that one is detached from their everyday use and meaning. They become the ingredients of pictures—not the things that perplex or worry.

Suppose you see a person holding a wine glass. Instead of thinking about what sort of liquid is in the glass—whether sherry or ginger ale, or whether the person's fingers need manicuring—concentrate on defining the shape of the glass and noting the twinkle of light on it, the curve of the fingers grasping the stem, the relation of thumb to palm and wrist. These are impersonal observations that lead directly to the desire to draw and paint the things so observed. To be able to make these observations you have to be detached from all other considerations, and this gives the relief of mind which is so necessary. You lose consciousness of yourself—forget the clothes you wear, how you look in the mirror—and become attentive to things outside yourself.

How do you cultivate this detached attitude? By *seeing* instead of merely looking. By making notes in pen, pencil, or chalk in a small book, always carried, as necessary as a purse (Figure 3). You have to be "above the battle." And life is so often of necessity a battle. But when once this attitude is grasped and adopted it becomes a great benefit and relief and gives new life. The world is so full of riches for the observer, so full of wonders. It is a small step from the observer to the creator, and those who wish to paint have only to become familiar with the tools and then accumulate sufficient pictorial observations: these will then find their own inevitable outlet like steam from the kettle.

FIGURE 3. *Making notes in a sketch book.*

13

SIMPLE DEFINITIONS OF SOME OF
THE TERMS AND PHRASES
USED BY PAINTERS

FORM: This is a word that is always cropping up in studio talk or in any book about the art of drawing or painting. It is not easy to make a simple definition of the word as it indicates a complicated concept. *Form* in painting is the solidity of objects, the front and sides of things in space, with also the indication that there is a back, that the objects are standing in a space, an area, with air behind them as well as in front. Painting is two-dimensional, because it is the application of color on a flat surface, so the illusion of the third dimension of solid objects must be achieved by shading. Of course painting need not strive to give this illusion of solidity; it can consist of flat spaces of color laid on to give a pattern, as in most primitive painting and in some modern work that has been influenced by Eastern pattern painting. But usually the Western artist has a wish to express "form" by giving an illusion of the third dimension, and this is chiefly done by shading.

PLANES: Following on from the word *form* there is the word *planes* which denotes all the facets of an object— its front and back and sides; the solid form is realized because the eye is able to see some of the planes into

which it divides. Take a square box: there is the front
(which is in the same plane as the picture space), then
there are the side planes, and if the box were made of
glass the back plane could be seen. It is where one
plane ends and the other begins that has to be noted
when drawing or painting an object, be it a face or a
box. Round objects also have their planes, which are
harder to detect because the transition from "front" to
"side" is not obvious. The highlight on a round surface often gives the hint as to where one plane divides
from another.

SHAPE: This is more or less self-evident. Shape, for a
painter, is determined by observing where one thing
contacts another. Shapes must always be seen in relation to what is behind them, or what is beside them—
not isolated, on their own. Keen observation of shape
is essential before good landscape or still life painting
can be done. When you can define a shape, in relation
to the shapes surrounding it, you have begun your
painting in earnest.

LOCAL COLORS: Color is baffling to try to describe in
words. *Local color* is the actual color of a substance or
object seen at close quarters and in ordinary daylight.
Naturally *local colors* are those seen only in the immediate forefront of your vision, for with any distance
the atmosphere gives a grayness to the color and thus
diminishes its force. *Local color* is the color of the

thing as you see it when matching up a color in a shop; it is the pure color without any admixture.

TONE and HALF-TONES: *Tone* is one of the most important factors in any kind of representational painting, but it is difficult to define. Every color, apart from purely local color, has gray mixed in with it, from a light gray to a near-black: *tone* is the weight of a color in this sense—the degree of darkness in it. It sets the "key" to the picture—whether it is in a light key or a dark. To register *tone* out of doors it is essential to half-shut your eyes. Then the tone-depth of local colors gives way to the overall tone of the colors in any given part of the view, and your eye registers the degree of darkness in it as compared with the adjacent areas. Toneless painting, like toneless singing, is too light in its register; it makes insipid pictures.

HANDLING: This is the way you work your brush or other tools. It is strictly personal to the individual and gives to his work much of its unique character. Loose, dashing handling gives a sense of energy, and tight, hard handling gives finish and precision. Always remember that using the brush is like using a pen—let your personality express itself in the way you handle your tools.

PERSPECTIVE: Perspective can best be explained by a diagram and in Figure 4 you can see the rudiments of pictorial perspective. It is the process (or technique) of reproducing on a flat surface solid objects in space so as to give a correct impression of their relative position and magnitude—a sense of "recession." It is sometimes

FIGURE 4. *The elements of pictorial perspective.*

helpful to draw lightly an "eye-line," level with your own horizontal line of sight (which is, in fact, your horizon line). All parallel lines in the landscape before you appear to converge toward a given point on this eye-line—those above your eye level seem to converge downward and those below to converge upward. All parallel lines to your left or right converge to the same point—the "vanishing point," as it is called. There are all sorts of complications in advanced perspective, but this is the simple keynote to the whole thing. The basis of it all is the simple, observable fact that the size of any given object appears to decrease as it gets further away from the eye.

RECESSION: Referring to the view before you, this means its "going away" from your eye to the further-most distance. Plane succeeds plane as the object you see "goes back" toward the horizon. The further away from you an object is, the greater is the amount of atmosphere between you and it. So pictorially *recession* results in both diminution in *size* and decrease of *local color,* with corresponding increase of *atmospheric color* (usually grayness or blueness). In relation to the canvas, *recession* means the "going back" from the base line to the sky line—which will be fairly low on the canvas if the subject is a flat landscape and high on the canvas if the subject is mountains.

FOREGROUND, MIDDLE DISTANCE, and BACKGROUND: From what we have just seen, these words simply de-note that which is (*a*) nearest to you, (*b*) midway be-tween you and the horizon, and (*c*) furthest away—usually near or actually on your horizon line. Usual-ly the foreground is in intense colors (chiefly local color), the middle distance has a certain amount of gray mixed with the colors, and the distance or background has still more gray or blue-gray—or even pure blue, mixed with the colors.

CONTOUR: The contour of an object is just the outline or bounding line where its shape meets that of another, and this defining line is extremely important in painting. "Look after the contours and the picture will look after itself" was probably the constant thought of Cézanne, and how right he was. The contours must be followed inch by inch (look at Illustration 1) with the most extreme sensitivity.

COMPOSITION: The arrangement of shapes in the picture space is the composition of the picture. Artists speak of composition of line, of color, and of mass. Balance is essential—but not necessarily symmetry. To compose a picture well you must organize all the component parts into a unity. A large light mass can be balanced by a small dark one, or vice versa. Artists also recognize composition inside the space of the picture from foreground to distance as well as from left to right. The shape of the pyramid was frequently cited in the past as being the "classical" basis for composition—especially of portraits—but during the past eighty years or so painters have gradually broken away from most rules and there are now no commonly accepted formulas. Many painters rely solely on their own sense of balance and proportion. Skill in composition is probably one of the last things one acquires for it needs experience to compose a picture well, and this is won only by constant trial and error.

2. Making a Start with Sketching and Water Color: It's Easier Than You Think

WONDERFULLY vital drawings and paintings by primitive peoples have been discovered, which proves that many thousands of years ago the art of drawing was there, innate, in mankind. Everyone can draw, for it is an inherent human trait far more natural than writing. Unfortunately most people lose this power as they grow older, or rather it is overlaid by more complicated mental processes. It needs only the desire to reawaken it and the courage to proceed and rapidly the power to express what one sees, in drawing and in paint, comes back again.

So take courage and go ahead.

The first thing to get is a sketch book: not too big a one but a handy pocket size that you can carry about at all times. You can of course buy a children's drawing book for a few cents, but this has a flimsy cover and has to be folded or rolled to carry, and that spoils the page, so a sketch book with thinnish cartridge paper and a good stout cover is the best investment in the end. See that the paper is not too thick or too rough in surface. Nothing harder than a 3B pencil is much use. Get a black Conté crayon or black chalk pencil with the wood round it, for this is the kind of pencil that will give you most satisfaction in sketching. Of course you will need a razor blade or sharp penknife because the breaking of points is a very frequent occurrence. Do not sharpen the pencil to a fine point—just a blunted point.

Now you have your sketch book and your pencil, what are you going to look for? What are you going to start on? Don't start straightaway on a landscape. Just focus your attention on a few simple things that are before you in the room you are in. Something the *shape* of which attracts your interest, say a decanter, or a wine glass, or a vase of flowers. Draw a definite shape on the blank page of the sketch book with a firm, thick line—say a rough oblong. Count this as your picture space: into this defined shape you are going to put your drawing. Then begin with the part of the selected object that interests you most. Perhaps it is the bulge of the decanter—boldly draw the curve of the right-hand side and then look across and draw the corresponding curve of the other side; then go upward to the lip and the stopper, drawing first one side and then the other; then look at the base, the dark curve where the decanter rests upon the sideboard. You now have the shape of the object—then relate this to the glass that is near it; notice the size of the glass in relation to the decanter and repeat the process, taking into account where the two objects are placed in your oblong space.

When you are drawing flowers, half-shut your eyes and see the whole group of the flowers: don't select one and then add others, but try to see the light masses against the darker ones or against the leaves. Just sketch in vaguely the general group, in a light way, taking into account the size of the jug or vase in which they are placed. Shade in with a quick scribble the dark and leave your paper white for the light parts. Note where the flowers come against what is behind them, darken where a light patch meets a darker part by an additional heavy scribble, still bearing in mind the edges of your picture space; decide where the table comes in relation to the flowerpot or vase and give this a distinct emphasis. Just as you would arrange the flowers in the pot, so arrange the whole subject of flowers and pot and table and background in the space you are dealing with, namely an oblong of a few inches, arranging them in what you think is a pleasing, harmonious scheme. You are not dealing with color when you are drawing with a pencil so try to eliminate color from your mind and just see the things in terms of either line or scribbled dark and light, making things as simple as you can. You can make many attempts at the one theme, trying again and again until you have

FIGURE 5. *Pot of flowers vaguely sketched in quick scribble.*

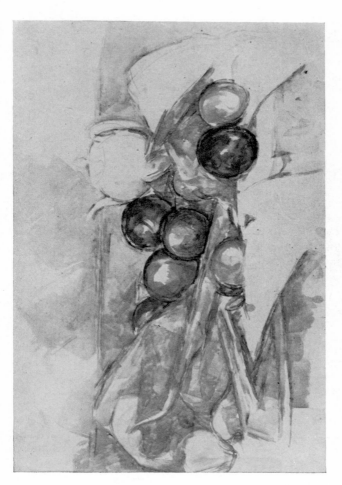

1. Page 19. FRUIT by Cezanne. Study the way in which the contours are delineated, and the forms placed one against the other, giving structure and solidity to the slightest sketch.

2. Page 35. STUDY OF TREES. Watercolor by James Holland (1800-70). Note the brushing-in of sky and general outlining, leaving foliage and light parts to the end. (Courtesy of Leger Galleries)

achieved a sketch that gives you some satisfaction as regards the placing and spacing and the broad general
massing of dark and light. I have done this in Figure 5.

OUT-OF-DOORS SKETCHING

Having practiced enough with these sketches of simple
things seen in the home, and feeling some confidence
in seeing objects as shapes and placing them in relation
to each other within the picture space, you may feel
some urge to try your luck at going out to nature and
sketching a landscape. It would probably be as well to
treat yourself to a larger sketch book, not too large, but
one about 8 inches by 10 inches, again with a good
stout cover—a cover that folds back easily. Those with
perforations and metal rings which permit the sheets
to fold over easily and to lie flat are ideal for the purpose. Do not take a stool, for it is fatal to sit down—
get into the habit of standing up before nature at the
outset. Perhaps you might add one or two colored
chalks to your pencils for this new venture: not the
greasy chalks but those with more powder in them—
there are very good cheap sets of chalks (pastels) which
are admirable for the purpose.

Now indeed you are out on the big adventure, for
there is so much to select from in nature, and a matter
of primary importance is the selection of the things
which can be portrayed in terms of your medium—

which, for the present, is a blunt-pointed soft pencil or a few crayons—and your drawing surface, a sheet of white paper in a sketching book.

So you are now out in the presence of nature: by road, afoot, or by car or bus or rail, you have arrived out in the heart of the country. Your modesty would naturally make you seek a spot that was not over-looked, that was away from likely prying eyes. You stop: there before you is a scene you love—your emotion warms and goes out to the essential beauty of what is before you. This is the place to halt. This is the scene of your effort and the chief problem is, how are you to convey what you feel and see on to the page of your sketch book?

In order to select from the view that lies before you just what parts you are to put into your sketch, it is a good idea to have with you a piece of cardboard, about the size of your sketch book, with a hole cut in it, say 5 inches by 3 inches. You can put this "view-finder" up before your eyes and through it you can search round for just that right part of the large landscape that seems to fit in with your idea of the beauty of the scene, and yet on a scale that can be translated to your small page. You now see that a group of trees on the right just comes in at the angle necessary to lead you to the haystack in the middle distance and the cottage building on the left just leads again toward the central theme of the rolling hills with the farm and haystacks nestling beneath them. So your composition is roughly settled and you can now begin on your sketch. Remember to half-shut your eyes, and always to take the big masses first and then work from them to the details. Scribble in the darks, leaving the light parts faint and the *highest* lights, such as the sky, your white paper. Then if you wish to make a note of color take your crayons and go over the sketch, putting in just one or two tints, giving the broad suggestion of the color scheme of the whole scene.

THE VALUE AND USE OF THE NOTEBOOK

From what has already been experienced there is probably no doubt left in your mind that the sketch book is invaluable. But in addition to the use of the sketch book for making drawings of things directly, there is another use that will be found helpful—as a notebook to jot down constantly anything that strikes you, at any time, as being suitable for picture making. These notes can be made either in written form or in simple diagram style and with written notes added about color or massing. The notebook can be just a tiny diary or a small book with ruled lines—anything that you can carry without noticing it. This should always be handy. You may notice the happy grouping of two or three people standing at a bus stop, the strong deep yellow of one coat contrasting with the purple-gray of another and "foiled" by the black of a third. You may see a large dark group of trees silhouetted against greenish blue sky and perhaps a cart track leading to the trees from a gate in the foreground. These things just need putting down ever so roughly in your book. It is out of the constant series of notations that you will gradually build up the pictorial vision; and you will begin really to *see* things—making all life round you of constant interest and giving you the wish to express with a pencil the things you have seen, first in terms of written notes or drawn line, and then later with added washes of color. You are on your way to make pictures for your *own* pleasure in the first instance and—perhaps, later—for others as well.

MAKING A START WITH WATER COLORS

You have made your sketches, you are keeping constant notes and you now feel a wish to branch out into a more ambitious medium. You summon up enough confidence to go and purchase some water colors and the necessary accessories.

WHAT YOU HAVE TO GET

First the paints. I advise starting off with a few tubes of water colors—just the minimum that will enable you to paint most things. The simpler the palette the better. The many new tints, with fancy names, are not at all necessary. There are, of course, boxes of paints in pans which many beginners at water-color painting use, but I don't advise these, as the colors are not chosen or arranged to your own choice or discretion. Moreover, the box gets messy and the paints dry. If one buys tubes, just those which one really wants and gets used to using, they can be squeezed out freshly each time and arranged in your own order so that you know exactly where they are each time. This is most important, for when paints are in use they soon get covered with colored water and become almost indistinguishable, and it is so necessary to know just where to find the color one wants at a given moment.

The colors I suggest you buy are as follows: cobalt blue, ultramarine blue, burnt sienna, burnt umber, viridian green (otherwise known as emerald oxide of chromium), rose madder (otherwise known as madder lake), light red, yellow ocher, cadmium yellow, sepia, and Naples yellow. As chrome yellow and Vandyke brown are quite fugitive I suggest you leave them out always and also black and white. These two extremes are useful only in an emergency, and if Chinese white is used it gives an opaque surface which spoils the whole effect of the other transparent colors. You can get any deep dark color with brown, red, and blue without using ivory black, but sometimes this color is valuable for indoor work or figure subjects. But I certainly would advocate that it be left out altogether to begin with.

Having acquired the tubes, put them in a handy tin box that shuts tightly, and do make yourself screw in the tops of the tubes tightly after each time you use them, otherwise the colors will get dry and useless.

BRUSHES

You will need about four or five brushes; these are an expensive item as, unfortunately, the cheaper types of brush are of no use at all. It is also no use having small sizes in brushes; they only encourage you to do niggly work. You will have to take a deep breath and go for a size 12 *red sable* and also a size 8—nothing under size 6. These are the round style with a point. If looked after well and cleaned and wrapped in a soft cloth after use they should last for years. They should be cleaned frequently by washing in warm water and soap. Put a little soap in the palm of one hand and gently work the wet brush against this, rinsing it constantly under the tap until it is quite clean up to the ferrule. You will also need some of the flat style in *squirrel hair,* ½ inch, 1 inch, and even 2 inches in width. These are for big broad washes, and their use will keep you from getting "tight" in your handling—in other words, they will give good big broad washes of color, which are so necessary to good water-color painting.

PAPER

Having the paints and the brushes, you now need something to work on, and the best thing is good cartridge paper which you can buy by the sheet and cut to any size you wish. I do *not* advocate the use of sketching boards or blocks. Many of them warp, and all are a nuisance in use. But you will need a drawing board to fasten the paper to, and for this purpose you can get a good three-ply board for a few cents—I suggest one about 23 inches by 16 inches. The method of fastening the paper to the board is very important. Do not rely on drawing pins. First dampen your paper and then with pieces of gummed paper (which you can get in rolls) firmly fasten the damp paper to your board. It will dry perfectly taut and that is what you need, for there is nothing worse for water-color painting than a wrinkle on the the surface of the paper.

PALETTE

You can get white enameled palettes or china dishes with special troughs into which you can squeeze the colors, but I suggest that you use a child's large enamel plate. You can get used to holding it flat on the palm of your hand, and round the edge you can place your col·

ors, always in the same order. The palettes and gadgets you buy are usually not large enough for the purpose. The ideal palette for the water-color painter has yet to be devised.

PORTFOLIO

You will definitely need a portfolio, one that will take your board and a few sheets of paper—about 25 inches by 19 inches is a good size—and it should have flaps to keep everything together.

EASEL

You can get a strong wooden easel, about 4 feet 9 inches high, at a reasonable price. Select one that has no loose pegs, for these are a nuisance. The simpler the make of easel the better, but it *must* be strong; remember that you have to stand up and paint at it and not sit down, so get the largest one you can find.

You will of course need plenty of water, so that a bottle with a good screw top, that holds at least half a pint of water, is necessary, and a 1 pound jam jar, which should have a stout string fastened round the rim with enough to spare to fix it firmly to your easel.

All these things, barring the easel and the portfolio, should go into a haversack large enough to carry the brushes wrapped in cloth, the tin of paints, the bottle, and the jam jar. You must make yourself as light to travel as is possible—experience will enable you to cut everything down to the minimum. You have your haversack, containing all your small things, slung over your shoulder, your easel neatly tied up, your portfolio containing prepared board and paper; and so you set forth. There is one other thing—you need "canvas pins," which are small pieces of wood with a pin sticking out at either end; you will need these in case it is windy, when you should pin the board to your easel with them. You may need to fix a stone to a piece of string and attach it to the easel to weight it down, or use any other sort of expedient if the weather conditions are difficult. There is always a struggle with the elements when you are painting from nature.

WHAT THIS MEDIUM OF WATER COLOR CAN DO

Now you have all your equipment for painting at home or out of doors, so we can look at the particular strength and weakness of the medium you propose to use. Water-color painting is governed by the fact that you are using water as a fluid medium. Water runs downhill, therefore the board with your paper must be on a *slight* slope, not too great a slope. You are out to govern the flow of your water, which is the vehicle for your color, down the slope of your paper. That is the art, remembering always that the white paper must represent your whitest light. From this it follows that you must have a full brush—plenty of liquid in it to make it "run"—but not too full, or it will get out of control. The next thing to remember is that you *must* let one wash of color dry before you put another wash over it—that is the tantalizing part of water-color painting—so the warmer weather is the best time for the out-of-doors painter. At home you can dry the tints off very gently by the radiator. Water color, by its nature, is fitted for quick evanescent effects, not for the full-toned subjects proper to other media: the quick fleeting effects of sky or cloud, atmospheric effects that no other medium can give. But there must be a lightness of touch, a delicacy of handling. Heavy-fisted work in water color is an abomination. See Plate 2.

USING YOUR COLOR TUBES

Put out a small "squirt" of paint from each tube, in order on your palette or plate. Start at the left-hand side and put out the lightest tints, your yellows and burnt sienna, then go to your middle colors, your madder and crimson, and then to your green, blues, and browns. Always keep the same order. You must know just where your colors are placed so that you could find them in the dark. Lightly draw in your subject

APPROACHING STORM: H. B. BRABAZON

This wonderful water-color sketch by Brabazon must have been done in a few moments. It has caught a very fleeting effect and gives the essentials with a few swift touches.

with a 2B pencil, then wash in the colors of the lightest parts with a big flat brush and let the water run down gently. Have plenty of soft rag handy and take all the color out of the brush with it and guide the flow of the liquid pigment—guide it into place, just the right place.

In water color always start from the lightest parts, leaving any pure white bits untouched by color. Gradually work up toward the dark areas and always remember that your water and pigment will dry *lighter* than it looks when you mix it up on the plate. Do not let your water get too dirty in the jar, keep throwing the dirty water away and putting fresh water into the pot, keep your brushes well cleaned off on your rag—let everything be as fresh and clean as you can make it, for a dirty-looking water color is no good to anyone. Remember that you cannot easily alter a water color once you have put a brush stroke down. So you must make up your mind just exactly where you are going to put the wash of paint and just what shape it should be, before you lay it down with the brush. If you happen to make a grave mistake wipe it out quickly with a clean piece of soft rag. If it is not a bad mistake, leave it as it stands—such mistakes often make happy accidents in the end. Look at Illustration 2.

MIXING COLORS

The primary colors are, of course, red, blue, and yellow. Theoretically, by mixing these primaries together, all other colors can be obtained. Red and yellow give orange. Blue and red give purple. Blue and yellow give green. The intensity of the colors used makes all the difference as to the resulting mixture. For instance, yellow ocher and cobalt blue will give a very different green from cadmium yellow and ultramarine blue. Experience is the only guide in this matter of mixing colors. I have included in the suggested colors viridian green, which is a wonderful color, especially for mixing a neutral tint such as gray, which is composed of red, blue, and yellow. By mixing viridian green with rose madder you get a warm gray tint that makes an excellent gray for toning down all the other colors if you wish to give the effect of a shade upon them. Try a few experiments of mixing your various primary colors together and placing them in squares upon a sheet of white paper. You will soon begin to see the various effects that the mixtures give. The gray tint is probably the most important of all colors to understand. Every local, or bright, color has its shadows, and these can be made by adding a percentage of gray to the color itself—if you want a cool gray, you put more viridian green than red, if you want a warm gray you reverse the procedure. Again a series of squares on a plain sheet of paper filled with these various admixtures of gray with the bright local colors will soon give you experience.

When mixing colors be sure that you have enough mixed to give you your required wash of color, in order that you do not have to stop and mix up more color in the middle of laying a wash. Have more than you think you will need rather than less. Each wash should be laid on freshly over the one that has dried, if you wish for a deeper tone. The first principle in the technique of water-color painting is to put down good crisp, even, clean washes of color—not muddy, messy ones. Plenty of clean water and plenty of wiping rags are the secret, allied to good big brushes; and, of course, plenty of courage always.

LANDSCAPE

Water color is just the medium for certain landscape effects, and it is therefore understandable that the majority of water-color paintings should be of landscape subjects. In fact the English school of painting is famous throughout the world for its water-color landscape artists. Starting with the early topographical pictures, in which artists painted detailed views of country mansions in their parkland settings, or recorded castles, monuments, and definite beauty spots for patrons who wished to have pictorial records (just as photography is now used), this art later developed into a broader and broader technique, until we have swift, fresh pictures of the fleeting effects of nature: windy skies with floating clouds, rain storms blowing up in the hilly country, sunset and sunrise, boats in sail on sea or estuary or river. It is naturally unwise to use a medium such as water color to give all the full tones of actuality, for its charm is in the very lightness and transparency of the liquid washes of paint put upon the sparkling whiteness of the paper surface. Look at Plate 2 for a good example of fast work.

It is always well to be prepared for the vagaries of climate. If you can manage to strap a rolled-up umbrella onto your easel it is a good thing, for then should a sudden rain squall develop you can hide your picture under its shelter until the weather clears again. If the day is windy, see that you are near shelter with a wall or thick hedge or group of trees to give protection from the gusts. It is unfortunate that these windy, changeable days are often the ideal ones for water-color pictures. Hot days of glorious sunshine are not really the best ones for this medium in many respects, for the very energy in the changeable day gives impetus to the painter, and it is the quick emotional effect that water color can convey so well. Admittedly on damp days the washes of color do not dry quickly, but that is one of the snags of the art, and one has to learn great patience from the outset. It is no use trying to hurry the drying or to start on a new wash with the old ones still wet. Every medium has its particular difficulties which only experience can overcome—trial and error all the time. The proportion of sketches you may start and have to tear up for one reason or another will gradually decrease as you gain experience, but never mind the tearing up—each effort that seems to be wasted has really been a gain—it is probably true that the failures are even more important than the ones that "come off" triumphantly.

FOREGROUND, MIDDLE DISTANCE, AND DISTANCE

You will remember the diagram relating to perspective (Figure 4). You are standing at a given spot: look straight ahead at the horizon, put your pencil, your brush stem, or the edge of your drawing board up to your eyes in a horizontal position. That will show you your eye-line. All parallel lines, in whatever direction, will appear to converge toward various points situated on this line, which is also, of course, your horizon line. Some few feet or yards from where you are (according to how much you are including in your picture) will be the foreground, which is seen in more detail than any other part. It also has more definite, distinct, "local" coloring than any other portion of the picture.

The "middle distance" is that part between your

foreground and your distant sky line. As your scene recedes from you the colors become increasingly intermingled with gray until in the far distance you get
blues and purples and very much gray in the color;
and, of course, the small objects are less distinctly seen.

Having used your view-finder, you have now a fairly
good idea of your "subject." You decide to have so
much sky as against so much land. Do not make the
space of sky exactly equal to the space of land. You can
have a lot of sky or a lot of land, but preferably not
equal amounts. Your group of trees will be on the
right, perhaps a large darkish mass, and on the other
side, more to the forefront, will be a sprightly young
tree that will balance the mass by its more energetic
lines or by its strong silhouette against the sky. You
will notice that, although much smaller in reality, it
rises to the same height as the large trees, because of
the perspective.

You must realize clearly what is your central "motif"
—the part that all the lines and masses in the subject
are tending toward. This should be some group of objects, shapes, or colors of especial interest—for it is no
use leading the eye to an object of no interest or even a
mere haze.

If you find that you prefer to have a very clear outline of your subject drawn in on the paper before you
start with your color washes, you can experiment with
an outline drawn in waterproof ink. You can get bottles of these inks in several colors. Perhaps blue is a

good tint to work with as it is not as heavy as black and keeps a lighter tone to the whole picture. You can use an ordinary pen with any medium-running, smooth point. Do not attempt any shading in this ink sketch but just mark the outlines of the masses and chief forms and shapes. It is probably as well to leave the sky and the far distance without any pen and ink lines.

MOUNTING AND FRAMING

As water colors are fairly fragile it is as well to consider the mounting and framing of any picture you may be definitely pleased with. You can cut out a mount yourself from fairly thin cardboard if you use a very sharp penknife and a rule with a metal edge. Draw in the size you wish the mount opening to be with delicate pencil lines and see that you have true right angles at the corners. The difficulty of cutting, of course, is in the corners, for you will at first be apt to overrun the line —but with a bit of practice you will get quite expert at this cutting job. A fraction away from the opening you have cut, draw again delicately in pencil two parallel lines round the rectangular shape, and you can fill in the space thus made with a very pale tint of gray or blue-gray or any light color that you think will "go" with your picture.

To "back" your picture you will need another piece of thin cardboard just a little smaller than your "mount," but larger than your water color. Dampen your picture slightly on the back and with a stiffish brush carefully cover the whole back with photomountant or a good paste, being particularly careful about the edges. It is as well to place the picture on a piece of clean blotting paper when doing this work. Place your picture the right way up just exactly where you want it to be on the cardboard "backing" and with an absolutely clean rag begin from the center and smooth out to the edges, seeing that there are no wrinkles anywhere and that the whole painting has gone down perfectly flat on the board; then place a heavy book or weighty object on it, first covering it all with clean blotting paper. When the "laid" drawing is quite dry, apply paste around the exposed border of the "backing board" and place this against the back of the mount. After making sure that it is correctly placed in relation to the mount opening, apply firm pressure and again leave to dry under a heavy weight.

To avoid dust getting at the surface of the mounted picture it should be framed, with *passe-partout* or in a narrow frame with glass.

3. Seeing Things—and Feeling Them—
In Terms of Your Medium

It MAY be as well to enlarge upon the rather broad generalizations made previously about the art of seeing life in terms of the particular medium you are using to re-create or express your views. In this case it is the fluid medium of water colors taken from tubes of moist color and used with pointed brushes or, for large washes, flat ones.

Nowadays the whole technique of water-color painting has been enlarged and extended. You have absolute freedom to do as you please. According to most contemporary painters, you should aim to express through your medium some new idea or new vision that you, and you alone, can see. The camera can so well record the actual visible appearance of things and report the multitude of detail in conveying the representation of scenes and objects, that it has become accepted that the main function of a drawing or painting is to convey the artist's emotional reactions, his *feelings*, about a scene or an object.

So do not think that you have to portray accurately the things in front of you. Do not be afraid to exaggerate, to emphasize, to underline and stress whatever feature appeals to you. You may think you are exaggerating hopelessly, yet when you look at the finished result you find that you have been very temperate—it seems almost impossible to exaggerate sufficiently. You see a line sloping down, you think perhaps that you have made it even more sloping, in your sketch, than the one you see before you, but standing back and looking again you may find that it is not slanting nearly enough. And it is the same with all sorts of drawing and painting—one always errs on the timid side, making curves too feeble, colors too light, contrasts insufficiently pronounced.

So do not for a moment think of producing a pretty water color or concentrate solely on technique—think fervently and all the time of your subject, of what is thrilling you and urging you to express your feelings. If you fasten your emotion and thought upon the subject and try to forget how you are going to re-create it on your paper, you will find that the means of doing the job will come to you as if by magic. You will dip your brush in plenty of water and mix up plenty of paint—whereas if you are considering nothing but technique, you will be so hesitant that you will use too little water and mix less of each color than you need. It always pays to err on the side of generosity. Meanness never pays in art. You may have to be wasteful, to mix more than you eventually need, to discard sketches, to try again and again. But it is the generous spirit that will prevail. It is as though art were linked with giving and not with getting, that the spirit must be moved to express itself lavishly, in order to do good work in art.

There are many things that you will feel you would like to paint, which it is impossible to do on the spot. For these subjects you will need to use notes and sketches from your books, and work at home. In other words you will be training your visual memory—helped by all the rough ideas, outlines, scribbled notes, that you are able to make.

HOW TO USE NOTES, SKETCHES, AND MEMORY

Memory drawing comes easily to some people—the more subjective type of person. To the complete extrovert or "looking-outward" type of mind, the power to memorize, when not in front of the subject, is very difficult to acquire. The chief thing to bear in mind is that you must put down just those things you do really remember and leave it at that, not overelaborate with details that you think should be there, but are not remembered. The simpler the result the better: if it is just

two shapes together, two contrasting colors, that is all
you need put into your picture. Do not try to please
other people—just express what remains in your mind
of what you have seen. For these reasons, the rough
sketches you make should be only of the main masses;
if you wish to convey action, just draw one line from
the head to the foot and another for the other leg—
catch the swing of the stride. Make another small
sketch, with a definite outline of the shape, say 3 inches
by 2 inches, which you intend to fill, and indicate
within this the shapes of the dark and light masses—in
other words give a sort of geometrical pattern that your
picture will form when reduced to its elements, a diagram on a small scale which you can keep in mind
when you enlarge your picture. Thus you have the
keynote of your picture, two figures with contrasting
colors and shapes that go well one with the other, a line
or two indicating action and the main masses reduced
to dark and light. See Figures 6 and 7. You can enlarge
your space in proportion and begin to sketch in more
detail the things you remember, first of all in black and
white with a soft pencil or a chalk and then with color.

Memory sketching can be very good fun and should
be kept as fun and not made overserious. You may
wake up in the morning with a very vivid memory of
a dream that took a peculiarly pictorial form. Try your
hand at expressing that dream on paper. Keep to just
the things you remember. The memory acts as a sieve
and the unwanted things are forgotten, the essentials

retained. Concentrate on giving the "feel" of the dream in your color scheme, and all its odd distortions of shapes or peculiarity of forms.

When you come to making a picture at home from a scene that you have had the time to sketch in

FIGURE 6. *Just catch the action you remember.*

detail in your sketch book—a scene that you had not the time or opportunity to paint on the spot, but which you desire to carry further—your written notes should be alongside your drawing. See Figure 8. Your chief task will be the enlargement of the facts you have before you. Use a sheet of paper which is in proportion to your drawing. Mark on your sketch squares in pencil, say of one inch (see Illustration 3), and then—if your picture is to be four times as big—make corresponding squares on your paper twice the size, i.e., two-inch squares. Now you are able to fill in the parts of your original drawing on the enlarged space, square by

FIGURE 7. *Remember the division of light and dark, and the main action, and work up your picture from that.*

square, thus keeping easily and accurately to the proportions of your original. This sketching-in process should be done with a 2B pencil quite lightly and delicately. You now have to rely upon your memory of the colors and of the intensity of each color. Try to visualize where the light was coming from, so that you have your darks and high lights in their appropriate places.

You may start with the sky, or you may put a light wash of, say, yellow ocher—using plenty of water and a

FIGURE 8. *Road scene: rough sketch for water color. Marginal notes in sketch book: "Purple-blue road, soft dove-gray sky, deep green-black trees. Make special note of curves of road and angles of telegraph poles."*

big brush—all over the picture. When this is almost dry you may put in your cobalt blue tint or a touch of viridian green or light red, or whatever color you wish, seeing that these colors are in their right places and

49

using the rag to wipe the color from the brush and dry off any running color. After the sky and your "overall" tint have dried, you may start on the land, or trees, or buildings, leaving your very slightly tinted paper to serve for your high lights and working always toward the darkest tints, which go in last.

If there are any parts of your picture about which you lack sketches or notes or even a memory picture, do not struggle to fill up these areas, but leave them as they are until you have an opportunity of going again to the scene or some similar one and then concentrate on making mental notes of the part or parts you have left unrealized. If such an opportunity does not occur leave the picture and call it finished—it will be a better work of art than if you try to force it to a finish by putting in things you had not realized.

FIGURE SUBJECTS AND THE HEAD

Figure subjects are undoubtedly difficult if you expect accurate rendering of the human form. Water color is not the best medium in which to convey such detail as is necessary to portray human anatomy completely. But there is no need to take this view of accuracy. If human beings interest you and they are the "subject matter" you wish to paint, then forget accuracy, forget that you have never studied anatomy, or muscles, or sinews, or bone formations.

People are much more critical of drawings of people than they are of landscape and this fact makes many beginners forego trying to paint people. Again, I repeat, take no notice of the opinions or criticisms of your most intimate friends. Just please yourself first, last, and always.

If you feel like putting an oval for the face, an oblong for the body, and two tubular shapes for the legs, by all means do so. If you compose these ovals, oblongs, and tubes into a pleasing pattern or arrangement on your paper and devise a good color scheme for your picture, you will achieve an interesting result. The prevalence of photography has given the artist more freedom to do as he wishes—to play with shapes and colors, and not to make accurate representations of things that the camera can do better.

To avoid getting overly self-conscious about painting people is the difficulty. Constant observation is the surest means. Look often and notice the line and shape of people. Exaggeration is just what you need, for when you exaggerate a line you come far nearer to its reality than you imagine. It is well to remember that people have sides as well as fronts, that the body and the head are solid objects, not flat ones, although this does not matter at all if your intention is to portray them as simple flat shapes. But the solid three-dimensional aspect is often the one you may wish to convey, and this is naturally the hardest thing of all when it comes to painting faces and people.

If you think of the head as a box of a certain size and the body as another box, you will find it easier to get the idea of their "volume"—the fact that they have sides as well as front. So if you substitute for the oval

Plan into Shapes
Keep in mind sphere, cube, & cylinder

FIGURE 9. *Figures.*

mentioned previously an elongated box and for the oblong body another box slightly larger and wider, you will have drawn the general form of the head and body. The legs and arms are four "tubes" fastened to the boxes. Thus you have your pictorial robot—the foundation upon which you can build all the complicated edifice of your complete human figure. The diagrams (Figures 9 and 10) of the head and figure will help. You can make hundreds of these studies of action poses, with the legs and the arms disposed in various positions, and in this simple way get to know the movement and placing of the head and of the body with its appendages of arms and legs.

Naturally you will draw the figure with clothes added to the boxes and tubes, but if you have the underlying idea in mind, the clothes will be added without much difficulty. Unfortunately clothes are often made to hide the underlying form of the figure, but with a little practice you can soon see where the body lies beneath the clothes and just give a few strokes to convey the whereabouts of the limbs and the pose and action of the whole figure.

In the diagram of the head you will notice that the eyebrows are almost halfway down the oval of the whole head—in other words, the brain-box takes up half the structure of the head, seen as a total entity. Too many people give the forehead and hair, from the eyes to the top of the head, less height than it should occupy, which makes the drawing lack dignity. At first sight, the face seems all-important, but when one considers carefully the proportion of features to the whole structure of the head, one soon realizes that the cranium or brain-box is extremely important. If the right proportions are given from the outset, the details of eyes, nose, mouth, chin, etc., can be filled in quite rapidly.

The next thing to notice is the distinction between the front and the sides of the face. There is a very distinct change in plane, although it may be scarcely noticeable in color, between the front part of the face, or

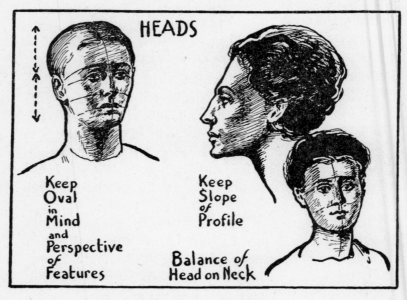

FIGURE 10. *Heads.*

body, and the sides. This matter of seeing the planes need not necessarily be overdone, but it should be kept in mind—and the change of plane searched for—otherwise the work will look flat and lack the feeling of construction that gives substance to even the slightest sketch.

TREES

The same sort of thing applies to the drawing and painting of trees. The fact that they are round and stand as solid masses in the landscape should never be overlooked, although with trees the change from one plane to another is even harder to determine than with the human face. A tree grows upward, with great roots embedded in the earth, and there should be a feeling for this upward growth: the trunk must not seem to stick into the ground like a pole or stick. It has been said that the amount of wood in the main trunk of a tree divides up as the tree branches out to the sky—the amount of wood in the branches, when combined in girth, roughly equalling the total girth of the main trunk, and so on until one reaches the outermost twigs—at each division the bulk of the branch is approximately distributed among the smaller branches or twigs. Look at Figure 11.

TREES IN WINTER

The problem of portraying trees without their leaves is most complex, but you will find it much easier if you almost close your eyes and look at the masses of gray that compose the twigs in groups, see the different

55

tones of gray, tinged perhaps with other colors, and put down the shapes of these various masses. Where the sky shows through them, they will be lighter and in certain parts almost as light as the surrounding sky —but not quite. If you make these patches with sky showing through the tree as light as the surrounding sky it will give a "jumpy" effect—so remember to tone down even the parts that you think are quite bright— tone them down to a slightly darker tint and the whole tree will come into focus without that effect of having "holes" in it which so often spoils paintings of trees in winter.

TREES IN SUMMER

The full foliage gives more mass, and the "solidity" of the tree is more readily discernible. Look for the groups of foliage, do not think of individual leaves, but concentrate on the patches of color that show the grouping of the various batches of leaves—put in the lightest parts, pale greens and browns, first, and then lead up to the dark shadows which are often almost purple—give the tree a pattern according to its growth. When you get to the parts that touch the sky you will notice that where dark colors come against the bright sky, the sky color appears even lighter and the dark a deeper tint, and that conversely where a light patch of foliage meets the sky, the sky color will need to be darker to show it up. The contours are therefore most

3. Page 47. RURAL SCENE: THE DOWNS. Rough sketch for watercolor. Marginal notes: "Overall scheme is a dull blue-gray, with spring corn green in immediate fields. Gray-green brown haystack (an old one) in central middle distance." Squared for enlargement.

4. Page 61. SKETCH OF LANDSCAPE: OSMINGTON BAY by Constable. This breezy chalk sketch gives the essentials for working up into a painting with a minimum of effort.

important. The outline of where the tree meets the sky, or the woods behind, or the fields—it is at those points that careful observation should be made, for the contours make the picture, giving the sense of round-

FIGURE 11. *Trees.*

ness, the sense of space between objects. Sensitive rendering of the contours is one of the deepest secrets of good representational painting. It is more important to see the way in which one thing (or to the artist, one shape) is outlined against another, than it is to see the thing itself. It is only by seeing what is *behind* an object that you can realize and express in your picture the shape of the thing itself. Spaces are of the utmost importance—look for spaces between, in, and around, the objects you are painting.

SKY

Painting sky is relatively easy. There are only one or two things that have to be borne in mind. The first is the fact that the sky is not a flat back-cloth, it is a curved surface. The colors at the horizon are quite different from those halfway up in the picture—much more delicate in tone—and the full intensity of sky blue, for instance, is felt only at the very top of the picture space. Clouds are certainly much more intricate and require special handling. Clouds have substance, although it is very flimsy and changeable, but they have form and shadow as well as mere shape and need to be rigorously kept in place. Always shut your eyes almost to closing before you decide how white a cloud is. You will discover that most clouds are a full tone less than white and have a lot of yellow and warm gray in them, as compared to the full white of any object or shape (such as a white flower or tablecloth) in the front of your picture, for the sky must always take its place as being behind the other things in the picture.

In one sense, the sky is a back-cloth, but do avoid theatrical effect. Handled theatrically it can easily mar an otherwise good picture. This is where you must exercise your aesthetic judgment in the placing of the clouds, so that they harmonize with the composition of the rest of your landscape. Clouds are fleeting and never remain for long in the same shape or color, but

FIGURE 12. *Sketch for sky study.*

you have to select just where you want them and keep them in the right linear and formal relationship to the other ingredients of your whole conception. They must not "jump out" either, in tone or in shape, from the pattern they make with the other objects in your picture. Examine Figure 12.

EARTH

To paint the earth you need your more solid colors, and you need a firmer handling. The only thing to bear in mind, and it is the reverse of the method of sky painting, is that the shapes, colors, and strokes of the brush must be more emphatic in the front part of your picture. They should become less emphatic and more delicate as you recede to the horizon. The very forefront of your picture has the strongest colors and the boldest strokes of the brush. As more and more atmosphere becomes intermingled with the objects, so they become less definite in color, for gray is mixed in with them, until, in the very far distance, everything is blue-gray or purple, with hardly any definite shapes to be seen. With the sky, the horizon is the most subtle in tone and the part overhead the most pronounced; with the land the foreground is the strongest in tone, color, and texture and the far distance is the most delicate in color and in treatment. The earth having a slightly curved appearance, with the bowl of the sky covering it, you get the two converse effects: the land receding from your feet curving toward infinity, and the sky, from the distant horizon, coming forward again curving over your head. Examine Plate 3 very carefully.

THE BRIDGE: JOHN CONSTABLE

This watercolor sketch illustrates a number of our points: the "sense of growth" of trees; the curvature and changing substance of cloud; the strength of foreground; the liquidity of water; fine lighting and splendid composition.

WATER

Water is as easy to paint as the sky. You have to record, chiefly, the atmospheric effect; its appearance has very little to do with form or shape. The only point to bear in mind is that water is flat and does not slant or slope or curve, except where the sea gently curves toward the distant horizon. But (apart from mountain torrents and waterfalls) in ponds, rivers, streams, lakes, and all inland waters, the level of the water surface is flat and parallel lines are straight, from left to right across the picture.

Reflections in water are usually slightly in darker tone than the objects reflected. Note carefully where a breeze ruffles the water and makes reflections blurred, or obliterates them entirely. Give an effect of fluidity, as a contrast to the solidity of your earth. Water and sky are more emotional elements and need more feeling in their translation into terms of paint. I have included a Constable chalk sketch for an example (Illustration 4).

4. The Medium Between: Oil Paint and Turpentine

BEFORE going on to the art of painting in full oil colors it may be as well to give some details of a medium which lies between water-color painting and oil-color painting proper. This is a medium which has many interesting possibilities. In many ways it is an easier technique than water colors. I myself find it most admirable for quick studies—preliminary tryouts before embarking upon a full oil-color picture.

EQUIPMENT AND MATERIALS

You will need a set of tubes of oil color. I should suggest starting with a very limited palette of the following colors: flake white or titanium white, yellow ocher, burnt sienna, cadmium yellow, rose madder, viridian green, cobalt blue, ultramarine blue, and deep burnt umber. If you are doing figure studies or groups of people in or out of doors you can have, in addition, Naples yellow (to be used with caution), and a strong red—say vermilion.

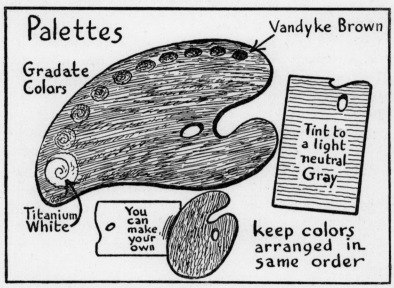

FIGURE 13. *Palettes for oil or oil and turpentine.*

You will need some sort of wooden or cardboard palette on which to squeeze the paints (see Figure 13). The same order should always be kept on the palette (and the paint put right at the top, not in little scattered squeezes all over the place)—a definite order of arrangement starting from white and going through the yellows, reds, blues, to the deep brown. It is most important that these be set out right at the top edge of the palette, to give all the room possible for mixing the paints. The palette can be just an oblong of wood or cardboard, not less than 10 inches by 8 inches, preferably a little larger, which has been given a surface consisting of two or three coats of size, and then a thin wash of a gray neutral tint, such as white and yellow ocher, mixed with viridian green and rose madder. Use will soon give this wood or board a lovely surface, for each time after working when you clear off the paint with turpentine and rag you will add to the agreeable surface on your homemade palette. The bought palettes from the shops with a hole for the thumb are very good, of course, but the thumb often gets numb and the strain on the hand is greater than if you just balance the homemade oblong described above, almost without noticing it, in the center of the outstretched palm, with the elbow well bent and kept in to the side.

PAPER

With this method of painting it is very important to use suitable paper. It should have a glazed surface that will absorb the turpentine immediately, but must not be too shiny. You may be able to get a good quality shelf paper that is strong and yet has the right absorbent surface. This may need some searching out. If it cannot be found, there are many printing papers that would answer your purpose. You might call on a local printer and ask him if he could oblige by sparing you a few sheets of "matt" (or dull) art paper or else—as this is unlikely—of *heavy* imitation art or cylinder-coated or perhaps even photogravure paper.

If you cannot get any of these glazed papers you will find that some of the heavily rolled artists' papers will answer to the purpose, but they are expensive and it is only as a last resort, if you have failed elsewhere, that these sheets should be indulged in, and then used sparingly.

TURPENTINE

This is the medium which you use, like water in water-color painting, so you need plenty of it. It is not necessary to get the expensive, specially prepared, artists' turpentine. You can get excellent pure turpentine at a drugstore or art supply store. It is wise to get a fairly large bottle and to fill a smaller one from it, so that you need not carry the large one around with you.

EASEL AND PORTFOLIO

These can be the same as your water-color ones. All you need do is to cut your paper to fit the size of your

portfolio, *when closed up,* and then have six stout clips
—paper clips of the really stout sort are just the thing;
place your paper on the outside of the portfolio, having tucked the tapes inside, and then clip with two at
the top, two at the bottom and one at each side—so you
have your paper securely fixed to your portfolio. This
medium dries instantly and therefore does not crinkle
up the paper. That is why it need not be strained and
secured as in water-color painting.

BRUSHES

You can use hoghair oil-color brushes with this medium—two or three round-shaped ones, sizes 3, 6, and
8, and two or three flat-shaped, with one large one, size
12. These can be the usual long-handled type of
brushes. They should be kept carefully and washed
well with first turpentine and then soap and water
after use (see Figure 14). They should be kept in a long
round tin if you can find one.

You could do with a strong ex-army knapsack to
hold your tin of paints and your tin of brushes, your
bottles, large and small, of turpentine, and plenty of
soft rag. You will also need a tin dipper, a fairly good
big one with a turned-over clip at the base to clip on
to your palette (see Figure 15).

With your knapsack over one shoulder, your portfolio with paper and palette inside and the clips out-

side, under your arm, and the easel in your hand, you are ready to go anywhere and start painting with this medium of oil paint and turpentine on paper.

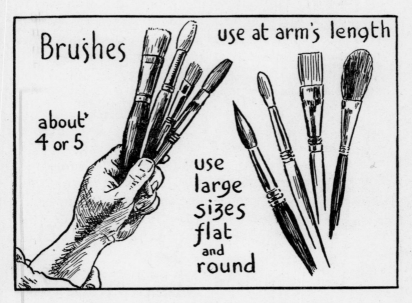

FIGURE 14. *Brushes for oil or oil and turpentine.*

METHODS OF USE

The chief point to remember is that now you are not dealing with a water medium which runs downhill and takes time to dry—you have the knowledge that almost as soon as your brush touches the paper, your paint will "stay put," you have no need to guide washes of color to the right place, and no need to wait for drying because the color dries almost at once. But it is not wise to put one wash over another as in water

FIGURE 15. *Dippers.*

color—you have to get the full force of your color straightaway.

The mixing of colors is just about the same as with water colors. The difference in use is the important thing. You do not mix up a lot of color, you dip your brush slightly into the turpentine in the "dipper" fixed to your palette, find the tint on your palette, and then take only the minimum of paint. Then, with very little of the required color on your brush point, you dip it well into the turpentine and rapidly apply it to paper. You aim at a full tonal effect from the start, for your colors will be fuller and stronger than in water-color paint.

One of the things to remember is that as you are using a more expensive medium than water to dilute your colors, you must keep the amount of turpentine in your "dipper" as clean as possible by liberal and constant use of your rags. Should your "turps" become really dirty, however, do not hesitate to pour it away and put out some more.

TECHNIQUE

Directness, rigorous selection, emphasis, and simplicity, are essential for using this medium, for once a brush stroke is on the gleaming white paper, it is there finally: no subsequent overlaying with other tints is going to help—in fact, this will spoil the result at once.

It spoils the effect if any preliminary drawing in pencil is made on the paper; therefore it is as well to take your smallest round brush and dip it slightly in your cobalt or ultramarine blue and, with a good jab into the turpentine, start off to draw your subject in a blue outline. Or if you consider blue is too definite a color for your drawing you can use a mixture of madder and viridian green. This, mixed with plenty of turps, will give a nice soft warm gray tint, that will make a pleasant start to your work.

After the outline is put in you can start with your darks because you are not working now from light to dark but in a direct full-toned medium. Your dark colors—ultramarine blue, rose madder, and umber— can be used, alone or mixed, for the deepest notes; you can then work in your medium tints of green and yellow and brown, with any reds or blues, in full strength straightaway.

SNAGS

The snags have been indicated to some degree. It is so easy to put on too much paint with this mixture of oil color and the volatile turpentine. And then you find yourself resorting to the use of opaque white and getting a thicker and thicker surface, which will probably lead to a turgid mess in the end. So always keep to the more linear aspect of your subject, choosing very carefully what you will put in and what leave out. Leaving out is more important than putting in. And remember to let the white paper do a lot of work. With this medium, as with water colors, the paper you work on is of paramount importance—I do not mean the quality of the paper but a constant awareness that the white paper is your ground and that it must not be cluttered up with any unnecessary lines or colors.

This medium teaches above all the art of *selection*.

SUBJECTS TO LOOK FOR

This is not an atmospheric medium; it is for quick summary effects which need a full range of color and strong contrasts of dark and light. It is stronger than water colors but it essentially depends on calligraphy, the swift drawing of the outline of things. It is therefore suitable for such things as farm carts or implements against barns, or colored fields, groups of people sitting or lounging at the seaside, for any subject that has linear interest and plenty of strong contrasts of color. Boats on the river or sea, houses, streets, animals, children, all can be sketched in with this quick medium which does not need the pauses and waits for drying, or the slow working up from light to dark by overlaying one tint upon another. Quick judgment and a carefree fluency are necessary for the best results. Put on too little rather than too much, keep always to the most simple aspect of the subject, whatever it may be, from an elephant in a circus to a group of fruit on a table.

5. Oils on Canvas:
Full-Bodied Painting Is No Harder

PAINTING in oils is probably the aim of all who take up sketching. You can give the full representation of anything with oil paint (or almost anything, for some of nature's effects are beyond the skill of man, or the range of man-made paint). You can give some of the brilliance of sunlight as in "impressionistic" pictures, or the exact rendering of flowers and fruit, animals, birds, and people, as in the work of the older masters, for you have the full range of tone and density, which, when added to color, gives all that paint can give. Water-color painting, as we have seen, does not lend itself to full rendering, but to an approximation or summary, with limpidity and atmosphere and freshness as its chief merits. Oil painting is more dense, more full-bodied, more complete in its rendering of the tones, the values we see in life. It is often thought of as being the most difficult medium for the artist to use, but that is really not true—it may be the most expensive, but it is no harder to practice than water color, in fact in some ways it is an easier medium, for you can scrape out and alter over and over again without doing much harm. A greater range of subjects can be expressed in oil paint than any of the other media.

One of the difficulties of oil paint is that there are so many ways in which it can be used. I cannot hope to deal with all the various techniques, but one or two of the chief methods will be indicated, those that are in keeping with the general trend of practice today.

Let us therefore start off, as before, with a brief idea of the equipment and materials you will need to start painting in oils.

EQUIPMENT AND MATERIALS

I am afraid that the necessary equipment for painting in oil colors is a bit more elaborate and more costly than that for other media, which is the reason, no doubt, why it is hardly ever taught to children at school, who begin with what, in reality, is the more difficult medium to handle, water colors. And also oil paint is a very "messy" medium to indulge in, for it gets on your hands and clothes so easily, and children do so love to get messed up with paint all over themselves. So perhaps it would be as well to start with an overall or smock which can be kept to wear when painting with oils and which you can cover with paint without having to worry!

EASELS

There are light portable easels in numerous designs, but the sort to select must be simple to use, without dangling strings or complicated gadgets for fixing. The best all-round easel, which can be used indoors and out, is one about 4 feet 9 inches or 5 feet high that shuts up to about half its length and is light to carry and that has good stout irons at the foot of each rod to go into the earth. It should be made of strong wood. Easels for use in the studio are of course much firmer, with a stout base, and work up and down by handle. They can hold any size of canvas up to 6 feet or more, but it is not necessary to have one of these pieces of furniture, as a good-sized portable easel will serve for use in the studio or room, provided that a piece of matting or felt is put under each metal-shod foot. Some beginners buy those small, slight, folding easels that you have to sit down to use, but I advocate standing up to work except under very exceptional circumstances, and therefore recommend a bigger and stouter easel that will not easily be knocked down in a gust of wind and that allows you to stand up to do the painting. So long as it is strong, light, and large enough to take a fairly good size of canvas and enable the artist to stand up comfortably to work, it does not matter what make or pattern it is—whether it is made of wood or steel rods or any other metal; although I find from experience that wood is still the best material for an easel, but see Figure 16.

FIGURE 16. *Folding easel.*

CANVASES

Canvases can be bought in all sizes ready stretched for use. You can of course buy the canvas separately and stretch it on to a wooden frame, either one that has had an old picture on it, which can be picked up in second-hand shops for a few cents, or a simple wooden frame that you can make for yourself. But usually it is simpler and more expedient to buy the canvas already stretched, as the stretching process is not easy and means buying a special stretching tool. However, it is all a question of expense and many a good picture has been painted on a canvas consisting of primed tailors' canvas or unbleached calico that has been stretched by hand when damp (with size and a coat of whitening) on to a stretcher removed from an old picture—the whole thing costing only a fraction of a dollar.

Canvas is made with various types of grain, or "tooth," to it—from the finest, smoothest surface to a very rough coarse grain, and the type of work you do will determine which grain of canvas you require. For ordinary use the standard "normal grain" is probably the best. You *can* get canvas which already has a tinted coat of priming on it, but most is pure white. If you choose a tinted canvas you will find that the color of it will influence your whole scheme of color in the picture, so buy it white, and when you want a particular tint to work on you can put a wash of color, with turpentine, over the whole surface. It dries in a few minutes.

As regards size, a good general standard size is 20 inches by 16 inches. It is as well to keep to one or two sizes regularly because you then have a chance of acquiring one or two frames for your usual sized pictures and you always have a frame handy to try the picture in when you have finished it, or when you think it is about finished. To see it in a frame will give you a new view and you will realize at once whether it requires anything further to complete it or whether it is finished to your satisfaction. Also a good size for a larger picture is 20 inches by 24 inches and 18 inches by 14 inches for a smaller one. If these three sizes are used fairly regularly to begin with, you will get used to visualizing your compositions in those particular shapes.

I have experimented with using canvas boards but have found that for outdoor work they are hopeless, as, however stout they are, they will warp and bend and become a nuisance to carry; for indoor use they are not bad, their drawback being that they have a harsh unyielding surface and have not the sympathetic response to the touch that a stretched canvas has.

CANVAS PINS

These special pins made of wood, with a point at either side, are essential. It is always wise to take with you, when you go out sketching in oils, two canvases of exactly the same size, then when your painting is finished for the day, you put one canvas pin in each corner of the used canvas, and placing the other (spare) canvas

77

on top, fix them together so that the wooden pins keep the two apart. This is the only practicable method for carrying wet paintings. They also need a piece of string or a strap to keep them firmly in position and prevent the pins from moving. (See Figure 17).

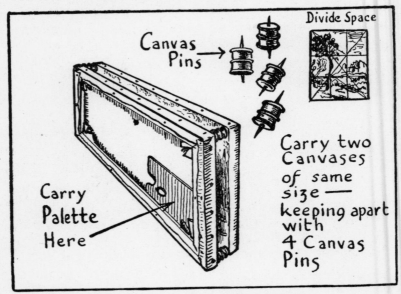

FIGURE 17. *Canvases with canvas pins.*

STOOLS

There are many good folding stools of a very light weight, but I do not advocate using one save on very rare occasions. It is nearly always preferable to stand up to work. You get far more freedom of arm movement and also are able to keep stepping back and seeing your work from a distance, which is of great importance. If you are sitting you are too near your picture and cannot easily get away from it to see things with a fresh eye, or, what is more important, to see the total effect of the subject in relation to your own rendering of it.

PALETTES

As I said in the previous chapter, it is both wise and easy to make your own palette from a piece of three-ply wood or stout cardboard. Suitably primed and with a surface of neutral tint, it will prove just as useful as a bought palette. It can be held on the palm of the hand without a tiring thumb rest. But for those who prefer a ready-made palette there are various patterns made in good light wood. I personally think the ordinary oblong shape is better than the curved, because there is more room for mixing the colors. A size of about 15 inches in length is quite large enough for most work.

BRUSHES

The best brushes for most modern types of work in oils are the hoghair, either round or flat. Of course, for certain sorts of technique, such as glazing and smooth work, red sable brushes, again both flat and round, are needed. The two sizes of sables I recommend as most useful are size 6 and 10. In hoghair brushes you need three flat, size 4, 6, and 10, and in the round style, one of size 8 will probably be enough. The brushes should be rinsed in turpentine after use and then washed with warm water and soft soap. They should be kept in a long tin or wrapped in a soft muslin cloth. At home they can be put into a jar of water after they have been thoroughly washed; the following day they should be taken out of the water and dried well.

PAINTS

It will be as well to enumerate the really permanent colors in oil pigment, colors that anyone can rely upon to be absolutely permanent under all conditions. They are as follows: burnt sienna and burnt umber, cobalt blue, viridian green (or emerald oxide of chromium), yellow ocher, Indian red and light red, terre-verte green, and titanium white. So most of the colors of your regular palette should be composed of these. Unfortunately you need one or two further colors in general practice which come under the next category of semi-permanent or those which have proved to be durable under most ordinary conditions and are quite suitable to use. These are: cadmium yellow, deep and pale, crimson lake or alizarin crimson, French ultra-marine blue (which, however, should not be used if you are using a lead white, but is quite all right if you have titanium white), rose madder, which is also known as madder lake, or there is the genuine rose madder tint, which is slightly more transparent (these are both about of the same durability), and, lastly, Naples yellow (this does not mix well with some other colors).

The only colors in oils which it is wise to avoid are the chrome yellows, gamboge, strontium (yellow), indigo, Prussian blue, and carmine. Vandyke brown, which is a very useful and desirable color is unfortunately not very permanent and should on no account be used in a thin wash or for glazing over other colors.

So I should suggest starting with a palette of the following, set out in this order from left to right on the palette and kept always in the same rotation: titanium white, yellow ocher, burnt sienna, cadmium yellow, light red, rose madder, viridian green, cobalt blue, French ultramarine blue, and burnt umber. You can, if you find it necessary, have a little Naples yellow and a very small tube of Vandyke brown, but *do* use these two colors with caution.

In oil painting it is essential to squeeze out enough paint from the tubes, and especially a good deal of white, for you will use three times as much white as any other color, as it is the diluting medium, like the water in water-color painting.

The best standard size tube of white to buy is the large half-pound tube; of yellow ocher, light red, cobalt blue, burnt sienna and burnt umber, you can have the slightly smaller "studio" size tubes, and of the more expensive colors such as rose madder, French ultramarine, viridian green, cadmium yellow and Vandyke brown, you can have the 3-inch tubes.

These colors should be kept in a metal box, and it is to be hoped that you will have sufficient strength of mind to fix the tops of the tubes on tightly, each time, after use.

MEDIA

Turpentine you will need in fairly large quantities, and this can be bought from a druggist, paint store, or art supply store. A good-sized bottle is required. Linseed oil you will need in about half the quantity of turpentine and the purified linseed oil sold in artists' supply stores is just the thing. I should not go in for the many so-called oil vehicles that are already mixed up from various ingredients, but stick to linseed oil and turpentine. As regards varnish, there is picture mastic which can be used very thinly when the picture has been painted a few months and is thoroughly dry —six months is better in winter or cold weather. And there is retouching varnish, which can be used almost as soon as the picture is finished and dry, in, say, a few days or a week after painting. This varnish is very light and colorless and is easily removed, and it will not hurt the surface of the picture. It is useful for bringing together the various parts of the painting that have gone dull while being worked upon. These varnishes should be brushed on very lightly, making a little varnish go as far as possible and using a soft brush that is flat and does not molt.

CHARCOAL

It is usual to rough in the main outlines of the chosen subject with charcoal, but I think that to do this with a small hoghair brush, using a little cobalt blue and plenty of turpentine, is better. Charcoal is a messy thing to use, and it must be thoroughly brushed off with a soft rag, or it will mix in with the paint and spoil all the color. When you vigorously dust off the charcoal you are inclined to leave only a faint blur, making it difficult to follow your drawing. If you use charcoal, dust it off lightly, and then go over the lines with a neutral gray tint consisting of green and red paint mixed with turpentine, thus fixing your drawing. Some spray with a "fixitive," but this is cumbersome and costly and I do not consider it really necessary.

PALETTE KNIVES

There are two kinds of palette knives made for artists —one is trowel-shaped and the other is flat, with a

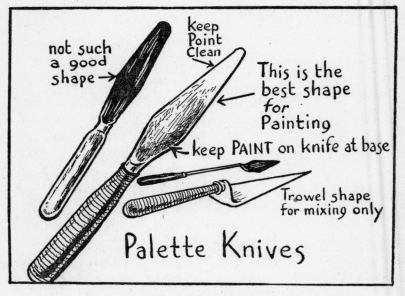

FIGURE 18. *Palette knives.*

blunt point. The only use for the trowel type of knife is to mix up colors on the palette—it is too unwieldy and too flexible to use for other purposes; but the flat type of knife, which should not be too long (about 5

inches), is a very useful tool for all sorts of purposes—
for example, scraping off, mixing, and even painting
the picture, as I shall describe in my subsequent pages
on "Palette-Knife Technique." See Figure 18.

KNAPSACK

All one's loose equipment—brushes, canvas pins,
paints, turpentine, linseed oil, rags—should go into a
knapsack (of good size, strong, and with a pocket in
front), which can be slung over the shoulder. This
leaves the easel and the two equal-sized canvases to be
carried separately—the palette can be fitted in at the
back of one of the canvases. Fitted-up wooden paint
boxes, with slots for boards or canvas and metal parts
to hold paints, media, and brushes, are of course made
in all sorts of sizes and styles, from the simple to the
most luxurious. I do not favor them in practice nearly
as much as the knapsack slung over the shoulder, because this leaves the hands free to deal with easel and
canvases. If you buy a fitted box, there is a danger that
you will feel yourself tied down to use only the one
size of canvas—that which fits into the box. You will
avoid this pitfall if you have a knapsack and carry
separate canvases.

MAKING A START WITH OIL PAINTS

If you tried out the oils-and-turpentine-on-paper method, you will be, to a certain extent, familiar with oil paints and ready to carry the use of them a step further. About the handiest size of canvas to start with is probably 12 inches by 10 inches, for it is not wise to start with too large a space to fill, and on the other hand a very small size is just cramping and leads to "finicky" little dabs of paint. Don't forget to squeeze out a generous amount of each color of paint on to your palette, arranged in the definite order already referred to in giving the list of paints required. The amount of white you will need will be at least three times that of the other colors, so give an extra generous squeeze to the tube of white. Keep the paints well to the top of the palette to give all the room possible for mixing the colors. Put the caps back on each tube after squeezing—if you make a regular habit of doing this it will save a lot of paint in the end.

If you have your view-finder with you, see that the rectangular hole in the cardboard is in proportion to your canvas shape—when you think you have spotted a likely subject, hold your "view-finder" before you at almost arm's length and note where the objects come in relation to one another; note also how much sky and how much foreground you need to compose a good picture. Do not hurry over these preliminary tests—it is so easy to rush off and start, only to find that the portion of the landscape you have chosen to draw and paint is badly balanced (either from side to side, or in the relative proportions of foreground, middle distance, and sky). Avoid equal divisions. If you decide to rough in the general drawing first, in charcoal, then do so lightly and flick off all the superfluous charcoal dust with a soft rag, before you begin to paint. It is as well to go over your faint charcoal lines with a pointed sable brush dipped in turpentine and using a light blue or a mixture of green and red. Then you have a definite outline established on your canvas. I don't think I mentioned, when giving a list of equipment necessary, that you will need a "combined" dipper now, with two containers together, one for linseed oil and one for turpentine (see Figure 15). This must be firmly fixed on to the palette so that it does not fall off when the palette is moved or held at an angle—this is done by pressing the clip turnover at the bottom very hard so that it is quite firm. If necessary it should be wedged with paper until you are satisfied it will not slip. This precaution prevents much bad temper and loss of turpentine and oil.

At the moment, I am taking it for granted that you are choosing a subject that not only appeals to your feelings, but that has line, mass, balance, design—in other words a subject in which the relationship of colors as shapes, as patches, makes a unity, a design that you can see will make a good painting before you touch brush to canvas. From the multiplicity of nature you are selecting something that you visualize in terms of paints put on the canvas, in strokes of a brush, side by side, so that the whole will make a pleasing, unified composition. But this question of the right choice of subjects will be dealt with again in the next chapter, so we will here concentrate upon the actual *methods* of putting on the paint, mixing colors, and so forth.

ORDINARY BRUSH TECHNIQUE

The usual procedure is to rough in the color scheme of the whole picture with fairly large, flat hoghair brushes, using only turpentine to thin out the color. You need not start with light colors—or, for that matter with dark ones—you can please yourself. It is a good idea to start off with the main center of interest in your composition and then work outwards from that —you can put the sky in last if you like, or, if the effect you want is likely to pass quickly, you can put the sky in broadly straightaway. You are now using a medium that can give the full depth of tone at once, so you need not be thinking of working up from light effects to dark ones, you can plunge at once for the full strength of your color. Remember to be light-hearted, not nervous or timid—you can never overexaggerate; although you think you are being very brave and daring you will find by the time you have finished that you have in fact been quite tame. So start away with all the dash and excitement you can muster—do not think of your friends or the people at home, just go all out for the thing you have seen and that you wish to express. Never mind about making mistakes. If you do want to change a color or shape, scrape out the paint with your palette knife and put on another color or shape. *Do not put paint on top of paint with either palette knife or brushes unless the underneath paint is really dry.*

When the rough lay-in of the whole picture, with the color mixed with turpentine, is completed, it will dry in a few minutes. When dry you can start again— this time with your paint mixed with a little linseed oil, not much, and a quick dip of turpentine. By the way, clean out your "turps" dipper with a rag after the first rough-in and refill it before starting again, as you will not want dirty "turps" mixed with the linseed oil.

Put plenty of paint on your brush and don't try to make a little go a long way. Keep mixing up fresh paint, altering the color and tone slightly according to your need, and place each stroke definitely in its place. Make it as nearly as possible the shape and size that will "draw" what you want to convey: as if you were laying many small pieces of stone to make a mosaic, each one fitting into its place with the others, making a kind of jig-saw that comes out in the end as the finished picture. After the first day, when you have gone all over the

canvas and painted a fairly complete picture, if you
feel dissatisfied but still keen to continue on another
day, the best plan is to scrape off the top paint with
the palette knife and leave a "smirred" version of the
whole picture. This should dry in a few days. When
you start again, just rub the canvas over with a very
thin coat of linseed oil and repaint your picture from
beginning to end. This seems hard, but it is definitely
advisable. Where each day is so different in atmosphere
and color from the previous day it is better to do the
picture entirely afresh than to try to repaint certain
parts.

PALETTE KNIFE TECHNIQUE

This more or less specialized technique is my own personal favorite which I have developed over the course
of the years. It suits my particular vision of life and
nature and has the great advantage of keeping the
color fresh and clean, for one does not use any medium
once the first rough-in has been made with turpentine
and thin paint (see Illustration 5, "Thames at Vauxhall" and also the frontispiece).

Here is a tip about the palette knife itself. Do not
clean off all the paint from the blade. Keep the top
half-inch quite clean and then leave a slight amount of
paint, getting thicker toward the handle, until a thick
"wodge" of paint has accumulated at the base of the

blade. Hold the knife with your thumb on this thick dry paint, leaving the point the only flexible part of the knife.

A perfectly clean knife is too flexible and cannot give the subtle effects that can be obtained with a knife which has been worn into use over the course of time. So look after your favorite palette knife: it will take some time to accumulate the required covering of paint on a new one.

Of course you cannot get the detail of drawing with a palette knife that you can with a brush. But that is one of its advantages, in a way, as it makes you "broad" in your treatment and prevents you from overloading the picture with excessive detail.

Should you wish to make any alteration, scrape out the offending part before you repaint. Use plenty of paint at all times, but alter the thickness according to the subject. For instance, the sky can usually be in thinner paint than the rest, and to achieve this, you should use the side of the knife, rather than the point. Once you have finished your preliminary painting with brushes you then rely entirely on your palette knife to finish the picture—do not leave parts of the canvas with brush work and others with palette knife painting, but make the whole complete, whichever tools you use.

COLORS AND COLOR MIXING

Anything to do with color is so entirely a personal matter, concerned with each individual's reactions and sensations, that very little can be passed on from teacher to student concerning the use of colors. The best plan is to go entirely by your own reactions—if you see the subject in a heightened, vivid color scheme, then put on the full strength of the color straight from the tubes. If, on the other hand, you see the subject in delicate pastel shades of misty tints, then obtain the softness and delicacy, by mixing white, blue, and gray with the colors.

One of the chief things to bear in mind is that each strong primary color—yellow, blue, or red—has its corresponding gray in the shadow. So we speak of yellow-gray, blue-gray, and red-gray. Gray can be obtained quickly by mixing viridian green with rose madder: gray is really a mixture of yellow, blue, and red, but in the green you have yellow and blue already mixed, and this viridian tint is most admirable for giving a delightful gray when mixed with almost any sort of red—although for a straightforward, pure gray, rose madder is probably the best red to use. If you require a cool gray use more viridian than red or put some blue in the mixture, but if you wish for a warm gray add more rose madder. If the gray is on the brownish side, use a dash of yellow with your green and red. As you can guess, the use of gray is very important in oil painting, for it gives the shadow which is always present in the color. In bright light the shadows are naturally most pronounced. Only practice and experience can give the knowledge of mixing colors and their shadows, but it is surprising how quickly this knowledge comes and how soon it becomes almost an instinct. You find that very soon the hand goes out to the right color, and the right mixture and tone are found, almost without conscious thought the mixture is achieved and the tone obtained.

6. Selecting Your Subjects:
Seeing Trees as Men Walking

As I HAVE hinted on previous pages, the selection of a subject is of paramount importance in painting any picture. So often good painting has been spoiled by silly choice of subject. It is quite true that almost anything will make a subject for the painter, and I am by no means trying to say that you should select some picturesque piece or some sentimental scene. The whole matter boils down to this—that the subject must have in it line, mass, color, in certain proportions that will make a good combination when translated into your medium of oil paint.

In order to *see* pictures in life one has to cultivate the pictorial vision, the capacity to recognize in a scene the essential pictorial ingredients. It is no use looking for a pretty cottage or an old bridge and then trying to make a picture out of that whatever the surrounding objects or colors may be. Look first for a "composition" —a combination of line, shape, and color in harmony, in perfect accord.

As we saw in previous pages, the types of visual subject matter suitable for re-creating in terms of watercolor paint are slight, delicate, ephemeral. The liquid medium, the sparkle of the white paper, make it suitable for impressions of weather, of billowing clouds, of quickly passing effects. With oil color you do not rely upon the canvas color, for all the canvas should be covered with paint when the picture is finished—blank spaces of canvas are, to me, simply a mark of inadequacy in oil painting. The detail of drawing you can achieve in water color is more precise; outlines play a more important part in so far as they can be more delicate. With the denser medium of thick oil pigment, outlines are coarser and are usually given by a meeting of one patch of color against another, rather than by actual lines. So do not look for outlines in the same way as when you are painting with water color, look rather for the *mass* of things: the amounts of space that the various patches of color occupy in your picture composition.

Imagine yourself out in a landscape—that is, out in the fields—all is quiet, no obtrusive people pass to put you off your stroke. You feel that there is beauty all around and that there must be a good picture to be found or conceived amid so much that definitely appeals to your emotions. But the question arises, what to select from all that lies in front of you? That is the main task, to select just the right position, the right angle, before you begin to take out your paints and brushes and erect your easel. Be guided by your center of interest—see where the lines of hills and trees, of brook or stream, lead your eye. There must be a con-

Modified
Line
of
Hills

Strong
Treatment
of
Foreground

Massin
of
Foliag
Again
Sky

Lines
Conver
on
Cente
of
Intere

FIGURE 19. *A landscape plan.*

vergence of the lines toward a given center, and if that focal point has enough pictorial interest—that is, enough pleasing shapes of color to make it a live and satisfying center for the eye and mind to dwell upon —then you have the theme of your composition; see Figure 19.

The next thing to decide upon is your horizon line. Hold a long pencil, a rule, or a paint brush at arm's length in front of you, keeping it both horizontal and level with your eyes, whether you are standing or sitting. And if you are looking at a *distant* landscape which is fairly flat, it will coincide with the furthest boundary of land you can see—it will literally be your horizon line. Parallel lines above this will converge down, and those below will converge up, toward the vanishing point. This fixes the basis for the perspective of your picture, and you have only to move your position to left or right to find the most suitable viewpoint from which to take in the subject before you. Keep thinking of the big shapes, the masses of trees as they group together. Maybe at one moment the trees are all ablaze with light greenish gold and then a cloud shadow comes over and they become deep, dense, blue-brown. You must decide whether these masses of trees, so important in your picture, will be in light or in shadow and try not to be put off by the fluctuations of nature. Wait and select and get the scheme of your *whole* picture well in your mind, *before* you begin to paint. And do not keep altering your first conception as the day progresses. It is a good idea to have one canvas for the morning and one for the afternoon, for the direction of the light and the positions and shapes of the shadows change so much that only the most experienced can carry on with the same picture throughout the whole day.

Another point to decide upon before starting to work

97

is what proportions of your picture space the foreground, middle distance, and sky should occupy. Do not
make these spaces equal in proportion—either your sky
must be predominant, or your land. Foregrounds are
always a difficulty, because they can be so uninteresting
—often just a field of green or a hedge. Never undertake
a landscape unless the foreground has a definite interest. Foregrounds have spoiled many otherwise satisfac-
tory paintings because they are so often neglected by the
painter. Your foreground should have shape and it
should have the most vital color and energetic pattern,
for it is, after all, the forefront of the picture—all other
tones and colors decrease in intensity as they recede to
the far distance.

You are in the country, in the fields, you are searching
for a picture. Again I say that you must almost shut your
eyes—look with almost closed eyes for the big masses of
trees and hills and fields, as patches of color. That is the
only way. If you see too much detail you will make a bad
start from the outset.

The next thing to discover is the depth of color—that
is the "tone" of things. Weight, in reference to color,
has, perhaps, no meaning to other people, but to the
painter, it is very important. It is the heaviness of the
color, the depth of its intensity. If you have no sense of
the "weight" of color, the feeling for tone, you will find
it more difficult to become a painter; as with the ap-
preciation of harmony and counterpoint in music, a
sense of tone must be there, inherent in the person, for

it cannot be taught or instilled. But tonality is essential to good painting. The way to get experience in judging tone is to almost close one's eyes and note the depth and density of the colors and not the details. Some people think this closing of the eyes is only a subterfuge. This is nonsense, for the very act of translating nature, which is immense, into terms of a small canvas means a great sacrifice of some things, so I think the half-shut eyes are essential.

THE PICTURE PLANE

A great thing to bear in mind is that you are working in a specific and defined space or shape. You have, not infinity to deal with, but a canvas, measuring so many inches wide by so many deep. Into this given space, this little world, you are going to put your whole conception of the landscape before you. So something must go, something must be overlooked or done away with. That is the point that so many people, who do not understand the technique of painting, overlook. They expect the whole gamut of the things they see to be transferred to the canvas, whereas only a very few of the things can be given.

Remember, therefore, that your canvas space is your own world and not the world of actuality. You are going to create in this world, this small confined space, a picture of something you have clearly visualized from the great world of facts and fancies, which lies outside you. To do this you must condense, you must emphasize, you must suppress and you must exaggerate. So the artist does not faithfully follow the actual facts, but he creates a new thing by adapting and translating the facts into the terms of the medium he has chosen. An object lesson is provided by Cézanne in Illustrations 6 and 7.

COMPOSING A PICTURE

Now, can I help you to compose a picture? All I can say is, *feel* the general rhythm, place your masses in a relationship one to the other but not in set proportions. Get the "swing" of the landscape, the trend, the essential underlying structure. Exaggerate as hard as you can, dance round your canvas, let your arm be moving from its whole length, and step back constantly, so that you are not close up and just nervously putting on little dabs of paint. Let your brush be *full* of paint, full to overflowing, don't work with niggardly little dabs of color.

Please do not get set in your notions. Do not on any account be hidebound. Let your imagination have full rein. If you see a tree as "a man walking"—then let your tree be as a man stepping out. Do not be obsessed by accuracy, for that is the end of all creation. You can leave out anything that is not of sufficient interest to hold your thought or your feeling. The necessity for elimination of extraneous detail is one of the great discoveries you must make. Your medium cannot possibly translate all the detail of nature, and therefore you should try always to make a synthesis, a summary of the things before your eyes. A wall of a building can be without all its window spaces—you can see it as a shape and leave out all the little details of the doors and windows—that does not mean that you are "faking" the subject: you are making a synthesis which can better explain your whole conception than by putting in all the details, which would only end by distracting interest from your main theme. Painting a picture in oils is like telling a story, you must make your point, but you must not get lost in a multitude of unnecessary facts and overpowering details.

LIGHTING

It is as well before starting to take careful note of the source of light—in other words, the position of the sun—when painting out of doors. If the sun is behind your back, you will be seeing more form and color in all the objects you are looking at than if you face it. If the sun is in front, you will be looking directly toward the source of light, and all the colors will be merged and the forms indistinct, with dark intense tones in the shadows. It is extremely tricky to paint looking into the source of light, but now and again you get good vivid tone effects by doing so. Of course, on gray days, when the sun is hidden behind clouds, you can paint facing any way you wish, for all the landscape will be diffused with a similar gray light. This uniformity of light often brings out the subtle coloring. In sunlight the colors and shadows are very brilliant and intense, but they are not as subtle in their range as on gray days.

If you are painting in sunshine, notice the direction of the shadows and how long they are. As the afternoon progresses so the shadows lengthen; also they are totally different in length during the various seasons of the year. It is seldom wise to have two different sources of light in the one outdoor picture, and it is almost always necessary to hide the source of light itself. The full intensity of the sun, and for that matter, of any artificial light, is usually too strong to reproduce in the picture, as all other tones and colors have to be correspondingly subordinated. Great artists have put the sun itself in their pictures and also the naked electric light bulb. But these are the exceptions that prove the rule. If you are to carry on the same subject during morning and afternoon it is a good idea to select beforehand a part of the landscape that will not be too much affected by the change in the direction and angle of the rays of light, the constant change that is going on all the time, but is more conspicuous after the sun has reached its maximum height and then descends to the horizon.

THE PICTURE SPACE:
THE PICTURE PLANE

Your canvas is your world in which you can create what
you will. You need not take account of the ordinary laws
of perspective unless you wish, but you must have order
and relationship. As I have explained, you are perform-
ing an enormous reducing act: reducing acres of land—
even miles perhaps, onto a few inches of canvas; therefore a great deal must be omitted, or simplified, or
condensed. As the landscape before you recedes into the
distance, so your planes alter, and each plane has its differing scheme of color to denote its "further-awayness"
in space. (This is called "aerial perspective.")

If you visualize a series of lines on your canvas gradually nearing one another as they approach your eye-line,
you will realize that your various groups of trees or
buildings are based on these lines, in recession, and the
placing of these things in their space relationship is important. Do not hesitate to put a "straight-edge" up
horizontally at arm's length from your eyes—a taut piece
of string is admirable for this. Then you can keep judging how far into your picture space certain things are
in position. There is a sort of architecture in a picture,
a building up of the design in the given space you have
before you, to be covered with colored pigment.

Remember to notice the *angles* of things which come

into the picture on left and right of you, as you stand in position in front of your chosen subject. These angles will help you to define the front planes and the side planes of objects. These planes will have differing colors, according to the source of light, and it is these different colored planes which help to give solidity to your picture.

OUTLINES AND CONTOURS

It is often desirable to give a good firm outline to your shapes as a means of emphasizing the design element in your composition. Van Gogh used the thick outline a great deal without making it too posterish—but this method is only a very summary one, as, of course, there is no such thing as an outline in nature. A firmly drawn outline does help to make one think in terms of large masses of color, but used too often it may become too facile and obvious a method. To the artist the real outline of an object is where it comes into contact with the other things behind it—and in nature often one tone or color merges almost imperceptibly into another—being "lost and found," as it is often expressed by painters. So if your vision is decorative and your emphasis is on design you can use the outlining method, but if you wish to render more unobtrusive effects, you will not push the outline too far, but will "lose and find" your edges, one against another.

5. Page 90. THAMES AT VAUXHALL by R. O. Dunlop, R.A. Palette
Knife treatment in this oil painting is broad and juicy in "effect"
and does not give minute details. Note the contrast in strokes between the sweeping sky and the horizontal lines of water.

6. Page 100. Photograph of the scene from which Cezanne painted MELTED
SNOW AT FONTAINEBLEAU reproduced opposite.

7. Page 100. See what he makes of the scene. All the fussiness is gone. The twigs and branches against the sky have been unified, simplified. A complete whole has been made from a seeming chaos of nature.

8. Page 123. STILL LIFE WITH FLOWERS: Pastel by R. G. Holloway. Even in this monochrome reduction something of the breadth of treatment can be guessed—the cross-hatching of colors rather than smudging; the use of darks to bring out the contours of the shapes. The main group is distinct, yet backed-up by the remaining objects in the collection.

Contours as distinct from outlines are a far more important thing for the oil painter. Outlines are a more or less simple matter, but to follow the contours of objects as they touch one another is an essential part of the technique of good painting. It is an almost invariable rule that where a light patch of color meets another, and darker, patch, the color immediately behind the light color seems even darker—much darker usually, in order to throw out into relief the light color in front. The reverse holds good also, for where a dark tint comes against a light one, the light tone appears to be heightened, giving again that sense of contrast, of showing up the dark shape. This constant fluctuation of the contours round all objects or shapes in a picture, gives *accent* to the whole composition and prevents it from becoming flat and dull. So watch carefully your contours—your shapes, as one object touches another, the *edges* of things, as they meet, *in terms of patches of color:* try always to be extremely sensitive in observing these dark-light, light-dark, contrasts.

Let us for a moment go from the fields and landscape to the room at home and examine "still-life" painting, as it is called. You can put together a group of things you like the look and shape of—or a group of fruit or flowers—and the more natural your arrangement the better. It is so much easier to study the contours of things in still-life painting, for there is not nearly as much fluctuation of light and shade as there is out of doors. Also the appearance of the shapes remains more constant and can be examined more closely than when one is fighting against all the difficulties of nature in landscape. To paint many still-life studies helps tremendously in all other painting, for you can master this intricate matter of the contours of objects. Follow round the outline of each object and see the altering color of the background—where light meets dark or half-dark, where darks meet lighter colors, and so on, emphasis being given here and relaxed there. Do not put in solid patches of meaningless color as a background, but strive for the feeling of fluctuating contours all through the picture space, making it vital and alive. In painting flowers, for instance, notice each petal as its shape meets what is behind it, do not just paint in any background round the flowers and hope for the best. The background must be full of vibrating color and interest, not just a dropcloth of plain color. Note again the direction of the light and the pools of shadow which do so much to bind up the whole picture into a unity.

CUBE, CONE, SPHERE, AND CYLINDER

Cézanne has been reported as saying that the whole range of natural forms can be resolved by the artist into the cube, the cone, the sphere, and the cylinder. And this is almost true. See Figure 20. From a tendency to emphasize the third-dimensional aspect of natural forms—the solid aspect, as objects standing in space—a great deal of the modern exaggeration of the solid structure of things has sprung. Many have, no doubt, overemphasized the cone and the cube and the cylinder; and

The Cone, Sphere & Cube in Nature —

FIGURE 20. *Cone, sphere, and cube.*

"Cubism," as a movement, made the search for the "box" effect in all things its chief motif. But there is no doubt that this cubistic view of things is helpful to the painter in oils. If you can visualize a tree as a sphere surrounded by air and light and a tree trunk as a cylinder, a fir tree as a cone and a building as a cube, you are on the way to seeing the solid structure of things and giving them depth and construction in your picture.

This new emphasis on solidity was a reaction from the weakness of the impressionistic vision, where form became almost lost in the shimmering effect of sunlight, and vagueness of form was a frequent by-product. But the good impressionistic painters always retained a grip on their forms and shapes and never became so involved in the sunshine as to lose the compact design of their pictures. This criticism of impressionists has been much overdone by critics of the modern school and there is still a tendency to decry the work of these wonderful masters of landscape painting, who brought light, air, color, and freshness, to contrast with the dark brown landscapes of their predecessors.

EXAGGERATION AND EMPHASIS

To give an extra twirl or twist to a line or shape, for the purpose of exaggerating your point, is quite legitimate in all forms of art. It is an extraordinary thing that, in painting, any form of exaggeration is thought, by some, to be absurd, while these very same critics will accept such exaggerations in poetry or the short story as quite legitimate. Fortunately, artists today have all the freedom of the poets and writers, to give distortion of shape or color, if, by doing so, they are making their point more accurately in accordance with their conception.

As I have said before, one cannot really exaggerate easily —it is usual to underestimate the curve of a line or the sweep of a mass—timidity is much more to be fought than boldness. Therefore be guided by your emotions and let your brush or palette knife give all the emphasis it can, for, by the time your picture is completed you will have toned down your initial impulses and modified your supposed exaggerations. That is a natural tendency for most painters, however experienced they may be.

PAINTING TREES

I am a little averse from giving definite hints as to how to paint this or that object, whether in still-life or in landscape, but perhaps a few remarks about the snags one encounters in painting some of the fundamental things in nature may not be amiss. Trees are so much a part of all landscape that they must be taken first. Trees are not easy to paint. They can ruin a landscape very quickly. Trees decorate the sky and vary from the poetical birch, willow, and ash, to the sturdy oak. Look first of all for the masses of foliage—or, in winter, for the shapes of the groups of twigs. See where the trunk grows out of the ground and diminishes in girth, getting thinner and thinner as it meets the sky. Follow the growth, follow the masses, and forget all the details of the individual leaves. You need to half-shut your eyes, when painting trees, even more so than for painting anything else. You must get rid of the little spots of light that filter through the foliage and not make them jump out as white blobs of paint to disturb the whole relationship of the tones and colors of the tree itself. It is a fairly safe rule that any tone of sky seen within the framework of the foliage of the tree is *darker* in tone than the sky itself outside the radius of the tree. Observe carefully the contours, where the edges of the foliage of twigs, in small masses, meet the sky or meet the other items of the landscape that are behind. This is always an example of the silhouetting of light against dark or dark against light; and this emphasis gives the "relief" or modeling of the tree.

PAINTING SKY

Painting the sky is a fairly easy matter and does not give the same headache as painting trees. One feels that it does not matter much anyway what degree of form or shape one gives the sky—it is only a light patch of color against which things stand—and that feeling of not minding makes you do a much better job than if you get all hot and bothered. There are one or two things worth bearing in mind about sky painting. The first is to remember that the sky resembles an inverted bowl and not just a flat drop-curtain as in a theater set. You discover by observation that the colors over your head, or at the top edge of the canvas space in your picture, are strongest and deepest, and those at the horizon are more tender and subtle. The cloud shapes have perspective and get smaller as they recede to the horizon except, of course, when there are big cumulus clouds massed on the horizon. There is light and shade giving form to big clouds, but usually the general atmosphere and lightness of the sky is more important than the actual shape of the clouds.

There are some marvellous stormy days when the sky is darker in tone than the landscape and the trees stand out bright against the menacing electric blue of the sky, but usually the sky tone is light with all the brightness radiated from the sun, so, again, you must half-close the eyes to register just the degree of lightness, making it neither too dark nor too light. Some of the great landscape painters have made numerous studies of clouds and the constantly varying effects under all conditions of light and weather. Probably water colors are the best medium for these cloud studies. As regards the oil colors to use in skies, never use a blue deeper than cobalt; and except when painting brilliant sunsets the yellows are never deeper or more powerful than yellow ocher and Naples yellow. Viridian green mixed with white and a very little rose madder or yellow ocher is ideal for the distant tints.

PAINTING LAND

The colors in the foreground are more intense than any others—it is a sort of reverse process from the sky. The part of the picture near your feet is seen in detail and the little shapes of tufts of grass, or weeds, should be acutely observed. As the land recedes, the colors become mixed with gray, and the feel of distance becomes mixed in with it until, in the far distance, the blue and the purple and the gray become almost the colors of the objects and "local" colors, the intense colors of the things themselves, are lost in the atmosphere that surrounds them.

There is a firmness about the land that gives it solidity. This means that the treatment should be more solid and less lyrical than in the other parts of the picture. The lie of the land, the movement of the fields and hedgerows should be noted, in order to give recession of line, as well as the altering colors. Things grow out of the land, and are rooted in it. It has rightly been called "mother earth," and the landscape painter should try to convey its importance in this sense. The main colors to use are the rich deep colors such as sienna browns and umber and red and yellow ocher—the earthy colors.

PAINTING WATER

Water, like the sky, is easy to paint if you have the "feel" of it in your mind, for there is no form, or definite shape, to worry you. Water is an emotional element and those who respond to its appeal can give the effect of its "watery" quality quite simply. Water does not curve, although there is a slight curve on the sea, as it recedes to the horizon, corresponding with the curve of the earth's surface. But usually water is flat and has to be portrayed in a series of horizontal lines or patches of color, in perspective. The reflections of things seen in water are most interesting to the painter. Usually the colors of the reflected objects are a slight degree darker in tone than the objects themselves. In very many ways the colors, as reflected in water, are more interesting than the colors out of the water—they have a certain tonality, as though looked at through slightly tinted glasses. There is constant movement always on the surface of water: the sky is reflected on its surface, the wind ruffles it and makes interesting patterns. If you are portraying boats on water, see that they lie flat on the water and give the feeling of having a keel down in the water and are not just bobbing corks on the surface.

After reading this general advice on the painting of natural objects you might go back and read Chapter 3 again, of which this is to some extent (and deliberately) a repetition.

PAINTING IN THE STUDIO

Of course any room in the house can be your studio; it doesn't matter at all about skylights and light from the north and all the old conceptions of what a studio should be. But it is as well to keep to the same room

where you can be free to leave things in a glorious muddle and put your pictures round the walls. The best
place to put a picture so that it can be clearly and easily
seen is on the floor, either propped up against a chair,
as straight as possible, or against the wall. If a picture
slopes, its oil pigment surface shines and you cannot get
a good view of it, so keep the canvas as upright as you
can. If you enjoy painting people and wish to paint portraits and figure subjects, you will be up against a tough
proposition, but there is no reason to be disheartened.
Ask any friend who will undertake the thankless task, to
sit for you; and keep him or her alive by talking—do not
get too settled and set in your task, always remember the
human element, and do not bother too much about
getting a strict likeness. Give your feeling and imagination full play. Self-consciousness is the curse of portrait
painting. Eliminate the personal element as far as possible—forget what you imagine the person sitting for
you thinks (or hopes) he is like—for this will put you
right off your stroke if you let it impinge upon your
mind while working. Remember to concentrate on proportions—the amount of forehead to the rest of the face,
the width and depth of the eyes, the length of nose, and
again the width of the mouth in relation to the rest of
the features. Also bear in mind the set of the whole head
on the neck, usually at a slight angle, and the position of
the ears and jaw. If you get the proportions of the face
anywhere near those of your sitter you will very rapidly
obtain a "likeness." It is a good idea to practice on one-

self. To keep on painting self-portraits is the best of all studies, for you know yourself and can take up the required pose at any time and you avoid all the interplay of one personality upon another, which makes portrait painting such a complicated business. Do not treat the background of a portrait in a casual manner, for the whole picture is the thing that matters most—so many portraits are all face and no picture. That is why you should consider very carefully the whole composition, before you begin, observing just what lines and shapes and colors are behind your sitter and noting how these fit in with and are knit into a general whole, that has design, in both line and color. See Plate 4.

In making pictures of groups of people, you need plenty of sketches—notebooks kept full of studies of every type of person seen in relation to those near them, in groups—with pencil notes as to colors and a definite drawn eye-line, in order to gauge the perspective. Do not put your figures isolated on the page, but give always some indication of the background against which they are placed. Arrows can denote the direction of the light and give an indication of the shadows. It is as well, when enlarging up your sketches to the size of a picture, to keep to quite a small size at first. If you splash out on a large canvas you will find so many parts of the picture that you have not fully visualized in terms of shape and color that you will have spaces of empty paint which mean nothing and only spoil the effect. So start off modestly with quite small pictures and gradually increase the size when your powers of visual memory are developed further by practice. Always simplify the folds in the clothes of your sitter. The main points from which the folds radiate are at the elbows or the knees, or any point from which the clothes hang and are stretched, such as the shoulders or the hips. Do not put in all the little folds and creases but try to pick out those main ones that give an indication of the form and movement of the body or limbs. Always endeavor to look past the obvious and give the underlying structure. It is much better to be quite simple in your statements, rather than overelaborate. The simplicity of the child, when drawing, is a rare gift that is too often lost when the grown-up becomes self-conscious. But this simple outlook is the one to try to retain when painting any subject.

STUDY FOR GIRL'S PORTRAIT: R. O. DUNLOP, R.A.

Note here the including and the leaving-out process at work as discussed in Chapter 6: "Selecting your Subject". No unnecessary paint on the face or wherever the paper itself can play its part. Design begins at one side of the paper and extends to the other. Placing and spacing are the essentials.

7. Pastel Color Sketching—
But It Must Be Well Done

WORKING with pastels is not exactly *painting,* although it is called painting, as a rule. It really is a form of *sketching,* with *color;* for one uses solid sticks of color without water or oil. It has proved to be a most interesting medium and of late years has become a most vital, alive method of producing works of art, since the great French impressionist artist, Degas, did those wonderful pastels in his late years, when failing health and eyesight made him take to this quick, simple method of work. Pastel painting is the cheapest method of any to achieve full-color results, for all you need is a few sticks of solid color and a piece of paper. There are no brushes; no medium of oil or turpentine, no elaborate preparation of paper by stretching—just a few drawing pins will suffice to keep the paper firmly in position on the board. Of course pastel painting has been practiced for several hundreds of years and not always in the same free and easy style, or method, that is mostly favored today. La Touche, the great pastellist of the eighteenth century, in France, where his portraits in pastel were very popular, always used an elaborate and rather smooth technique by smoothing or rubbing with the finger or a "stump." Except in the hands of a genius, this method tends to be messy and blurry and lacks any crisp definition of forms. This is the sort of thing that, done badly, has given pastels a bad name among artists. For to use this inexpensive and simple medium well is not as easy as you might think.

But there is no doubt that the use of pastels is ideal for making quick notes of all sorts of effects that need color. You carry your colors with you in a small pocket-size box and you can buy a small sketch book made up with colored papers of a suitable surface for taking the pastel crayons. It is for this reason that almost every artist uses pastels to make quick vital records of clouds, sunsets, or any subject where the color element is of the greatest importance.

MATERIALS AND EQUIPMENT

As I have said, there are very few things one needs. There are the pastels themselves: solid sticks of color with a covering of waxed paper almost to the top. It is wise to keep this covering paper intact as long as possible, for once it tears and is gone the pastel breaks up quickly. That is the chief difficulty about pastels; they break so very easily and get all smudged and smeared with powdered color, that you cannot tell, at a glance, just which color you are picking up. While you may treat yourself to the more expensive French pastels for special purposes, or to a few particular colors on occasion, the standard pastels are eminently suitable for general use. They should be purchased in a small wooden or tin box. A large box is not desirable. Usually there is a good range of the necessary colors in these smaller boxes, but after you have once bought a box, you can add your special favorite colors, as time goes on. You will probably find the colors wrapped in cotton wool in little niches— do keep them in their wool and their separate niches, as far as you possibly can, for pastels are so fragile that they must have devoted care if you are not to get into an awful muddle when you are trying to find a particular color. You should aim to keep the color stick intact as long as possible and to let the color of the stick be recognizable at a quick glance.

PAPER

The choice of the paper or board on which you are to work is probably the most important part of the technique of pastel painting. First of all you need a toned paper—in other words it must be of a color, *not* white, but the color of the paper must be subtle and not too obvious in tint. Therefore a delicate blue-gray—or pink-gray or a slight fawn—would perhaps meet most occasions, but it is as well to have a good range of colored papers or boards, in order to choose the right tone for your particular sketch. The "tooth" or grain of the paper must be just right. It is good fun searching round art shops or friendly printers' to get the necessary papers to suit your subject and your style of work. Printers often have a few spare sheets of "cover" papers which are admirable for the purpose. Cut your paper up into the size you wish to make your sketches and keep the sheets flat, in a portfolio, with a heavy weight on top. A useful size is 18 inches by 14 inches.

PORTFOLIO

Of course you will need a portfolio to carry your paper and a drawing board of about 20 inches by 16 inches to pin the paper to—a thin board will do quite well as you will not put much strain or stress on it, through usage, as you do when using water colors. In fact, a stout piece of cardboard or a piece of three-ply wood will serve the purpose admirably. If you do not wish to bother about a drawing board you can fix your paper to the outside of the portfolio with paper clips, as explained before.

It is important to remember that every sketch you do in pastel is fragile and therefore you need tissue paper to cover your sketches—cut to the size of your drawing paper. You should place each finished sketch carefully in the portfolio, covered with a sheet of tissue paper, and put four drawing pins, one in each corner, to keep the whole set of sketches in place, to prevent rubbing and smearing.

EASEL

Your easel will be the same as before so there is no need to worry about that—you may find with pastels that you cannot stand up so often, and you may therefore find that you need a stool—one of those abhorrent things that some artists sit on—and that should only be used very sparingly!

MOUNTING AND FRAMING

As pastel pictures are so fragile, you must take very great care in handling them. They must be covered with tissue paper from the start and put carefully into the portfolio with clips so that there is no chance of the surface being rubbed or smeared. When you decide on those which deserve to be kept, you must see to it that they are mounted on cardboard and as soon as possible put under glass, either in *passe-partout* mounts or in small wooden frames. The whole idea is to keep them from the air and from being rubbed. It is a good thing to have a small slip in the frame, which keeps the actual pastel picture from touching the glass itself.

I, personally, never use—and cannot recommend—any form of "fixitive."

METHODS OF WORK

My experience has been to use the pastel medium in a bold and direct way—using crosshatching of one color against another to produce the required result. For instance, if you wish for a green, you crosshatch blue and yellow pastels, varying the color of the blue or yellow according to the sort of green you want. The same with red and blue if you wish for a purple, and with red and yellow if you require an orange. Working as you do on a tinted paper your sky is put in with strokes of white and light yellow and blue, with a slight tinge of red where you wish a warmer tone. This direct use of the pastel chalks without smudging or merging gives a very vivid effect. The whole idea is to keep the picture fresh and spontaneous. You cannot alter pastels easily, once you have put on a stroke of color, so try to get the effect straightaway. If you do happen to get the wrong color do not try to erase it, but put other colors on top, with a heavier stroke of the wrist—making the colors merge by pressure of one on the top of the other. As you can imagine, it is very easy to overdo the pressure you exert

and you find that the pastel breaks up into little pieces
—so the skill rests in exerting just the right degree of
pressure. Using pastels is more in the nature of drawing than of painting, because each stroke is a broad line
and not a patch, as when using brushes and a tactile substance. The way to keep a certain amount of point on
the pastel to give precision to the stroke is to use the
sides rather than the top and so keep a degree of "edge."
You cannot sharpen the pastel as a general rule, so you
must rely on keeping an edge by the way you use the
stick of color. You are really making a colored summary
of your subject and not any exact rendering of all its
complications. Have a look at the pastel by R. G. Holloway, Illustration 8.

SUBJECTS

It follows from these remarks about methods and treatment that the choice of subjects for pastel painting is
quite different from that for oil or water-color pictures. You seek for big, simple color schemes, rather
than any detail, and there must be plenty of linear
rhythm in the subject. It is a cross between painting
and drawing—you have color to mass and arrange, and
as you are working with solid pieces of color, without
any fluid, so you choose subjects that give scope for
bold drawing and bold coloring. The use of a toned
paper also affects the choice of subject, for you are not

giving sparkle, or limpidity, but brilliant gay colors related to the foundation tone of the paper you are using.

GENERAL SUMMARY

It may be as well to recapitulate what has already been written, in a simple form, to clarify matters. I have therefore imagined a questioner who asks me twenty questions, bearing on the points I have tried to explain in the foregoing pages.

8. Twenty Questions and Twenty Answers
for Those About to Begin

1st Question: As a complete tyro, who loves pictures, is it worth while for me to try to start painting, irrespective of age?

Answer: The answer is an immediate "Yes." It is certainly very much worth while, from many points of view. The gift of being able to express oneself in terms of line and color is never completely lacking, but only dormant and overlaid by interest in other things that develop as life goes on. All that is really necessary is the strong wish or desire to paint and draw. It may come at any time or age in one's life. A certain amount of regular practice is all that is required, plus the sustained wish to proceed. It is a question of seeing life in terms of the medium of expression: of seeing lines, masses, pattern, shape in things as you look at them. Once this habit of really seeing things is formed you will quickly learn to express the things you see. Actually the means of expression, the technique, is not a difficult thing in its elementary terms. It may sound difficult when expressed in words, or seem difficult when one is looking at world masterpieces of art, but it really remains within the scope of all who have the interest to pursue it. And the benefits derived from finding this creative means of expression are tremendous. It gives an added interest to every walk you take, to every ride in bus or train, to every visit to a strange place. The power to *see* things with your own individual viewpoint is the awakening of a new world for you, which has hitherto been overlaid by reading books and looking at films, and sports, where other artists are providing the spectacle. The creation of a work of art, however simple and unsophisticated, is a help to your individual personality, it gives a new sense of self-confidence, a fresh realization of your own power.

2nd Question: What medium do you consider is the best to start using, in the search for self-expression through art?

Answer: The answer to this question is rather complicated. Sketching with a pencil or chalk is the simplest way to begin, but it is tentative and not very satisfying, although one should keep a notebook or sketch book handy at all times. Water colors are usually the first to be used in schools, because of their cheapness and apparent easiness of handling. But, as a matter of sober fact, water colors are not an easy medium to use, and their difficulties often put the student or beginner off further efforts. I would suggest that oil colors should be tackled right away, although this is not the order in which they appear in this book. Drawing and painting should never be separated; they are one and the same—every brush stroke should "draw" as well as lay on color. Every stroke should take a pronounced and definite shape with a beginning and an end. In using oil colors you are using the medium that can give the utmost effect that painting can give, for it has all the depth and tone and color necessary. Once you begin to understand its quality as a substance and get familiar with the colors, you will find it the most satisfying of all the media to use.

3rd Question: Is the more modern outlook on painting a reasonable one?

Answer: Yes, definitely. All this talk about the decadence of modern art is absurd. There are all sorts of experiments and trials and errors—the young artists dislike the older men, and why not? On the shoulders of the fathers the sons climb, but they have to believe that their fathers are utterly wrong. The new generation of artists cannot worship only at the shrine of the past—if they did it would be the end of advancement. Modern art is as healthy as at any time in the history of art and it has given something invaluable to anyone starting out to paint: it has given a free road to do as you please—obeying the code of the road, but with freedom to explore, and to develop and imagine what you will. There has never been a time when rules and regulations meant less and when anyone who has an idea and the guts to express it receives more sympathy. It is a great age for the artists. Painting is not the prerogative of a trade union or a profession, it is a form of expression which all can use to their own good.

4th Question: It is often said that it takes a lifetime to learn to paint. Is it, therefore, possible to find any degree of expression, as a painter, if one can only give up a few hours a week to practicing the art?

Answer: This is almost the same question as the first. The difference seems to lie only in the time factor. Of course it takes more than a lifetime to learn all there is to know about painting, in fact it would take a thousand lifetimes and then the whole art would only be in its infancy! So we can leave out the time element. It is quite possible and not at all difficult to find a very adequate means of expression in painting, if one can only give up, say, a few hours at each week-end to painting. I should say that a regular average of *five* hours a week would be more than adequate to develop and expand anyone's innate gifts.

5th Question: How soon after starting to paint, as a hobby, can one expect to attain a certain degree of ability in expressing the view one has of life?

Answer: The answer to this question naturally depends upon the amount of time and energy one expends. But it would not take more than two months, with an average of five hours per week, to achieve quite a degree of ability in expressing one's vision of things seen. It does not do to have too much idea about advancement and achievement. Let these things develop gradually and do not be in any hurry or become overambitious about results. After all, every expression is an experience and is helping in very many ways to benefit the whole personality.

6th Question: What is the essential outlook which it is necessary to acquire in order to become creative in terms of drawing and painting?

Answer: In addition to becoming able to *see* things, instead of only casually looking at them, one must develop the impersonal attitude. That is, the power to drop all associations that normally crop up and instead to consider the things one sees with complete detachment. Instead of seeing the cup of tea as a beverage to drink one has to see the shape of the cup against the saucer, the color of the tea, the stains on the saucer, the relationship of the spoon to the cup and the saucer and moreover the relation of the whole to its setting—the table, the things around and about—as a composition and design. It is the same with people and their faces. One has to see them suddenly, removed from all associations of friendship or intimacy, and

just concentrate upon the shape and color of their features—the mass of the hair, the general spacing and proportion of the build of their features. It is a sort of
detachment from the ordinary world, a sitting back
and taking note of the things that usually pass one by
—a child taking notes, as Burns said.

7th Question: Should we concentrate entirely upon
drawing, on trying to acquire proficiency in drafts-
manship, before beginning to paint?

Answer: The answer is definitely—no! If you separate
drawing from painting you will fail to develop all sense
of tone and color values. When one comes to paint,
after a course of drawing in black and white, it will be
like tinting a drawing with color, for the two aspects
have been separated in the mind and do not easily come
together again. All painting is also drawing, drawing
with brush or palette knife, because each stroke must
make a definite shape—have an end as well as a beginning—and by keeping the two things together as one
from the very start, you will find your sense of tone
and color values much more highly developed.

8th Question: Are expensive outfits absolutely essential in order to begin to paint properly?

Answer: Again the answer is a definite "No!" There is,
of course, a certain amount of expense when starting,
but if you avoid the made-up-ready-to-use outfits and
gradually acquire the necessary tubes of paint and

brushes and make your own palette and certain other things which are easy to make, you need not involve yourself in a very great expense. Of course, the things you do buy must be looked after well and treated with the utmost care. It is better to get good brushes, for instance, and look after them well, than to buy inferior, badly made brushes and treat them carelessly. Remember always to put the caps back on the tubes after you have squeezed out the paint. But you must not be too cautious about the amount of paint you squeeze out on the palette. It is at this point that you must cast thought of expense to the winds and become generous, for too little paint spoils many beginners' efforts.

9th Question: How far does emotion, or temperament, override the control of technique, in the art of painting?

Answer: It is always wise to consider your feelings as being the most important and necessary part of your artistic self, for without emotional response to visual things, no painting is worth while. Of course, there has to be a good deal of mental work also governing and directing the feelings and responses to stimulation by the color, shape, and line. The emotion must come first and then the head work afterwards. Technique alone will produce nothing worth while. That is why, when you are painting entirely for pleasure you should not get overworried about the technical details but go out boldly and strongly for expressing, at all costs, your *feeling* for, or about, the things you like rather than their exact delineation in detail. Intuition is exercised when mind and heart, feeling and thought go together, and intuition will guide you to finding just the right expression.

10th Question: Are such things as exaggeration and distortion allowable in producing good painting?

Answer: Yes, all these things which seem to look out of place when taken by themselves may, if rightly used, help in getting over your message. You must remember that you are not *copying* what you see in any literal sense, but interpreting the things as sensed and felt emotionally. It is just the same as poetry or a short story, where greater truth, more forceful point, can be given by emphasizing certain things and omitting others. These things should not be done as a fad or to be in the fashion of the moment, but strictly to enhance the view of things that you wish to express.

11th Question: What is the essential difference in subject and technique between water color and oil painting?

Answer: Water colors are a beautifully transparent medium and the guiding of limpid washes of color into their position on gleaming white paper is the chief art to master. Plenty of clean water, plenty of rags, and some good big brushes, are the chief essentials. You cannot put one wash on the top of another until the first one is dry, so you are limited in this way and cannot rush your work. Light, airy subjects, where the glow of the color washes are seen to their best advantage, are the subjects most suitable. Oil paint is a denser medium and can give far more density of tone value than water color. You can run the whole gamut of tone from bright light to dark shadow, and as you can always scrape off the paint if you wish to alter your picture, you can keep on working on your canvas until you get the desired effect. Alterations in water color, on the other hand, nearly always lead to disaster. The subjects one can choose for oils are far more varied; in fact, with oil paints almost any and every conceivable subject can be attempted. You can start straightaway with the full depth of tone and need not work up from light to dark as in water-color painting.

12th Question: Are the many differing styles observable in present-day painting a good thing?

Answer: On the whole it is a very healthy sign that there is so much experimentation in present-day art. In the old days there were only a very limited number of ways of painting a picture, but today you can choose from a wide range. Freshness of vision—having a definite personal outlook and attitude to things—is the essential. Each individual has a way of seeing which is unique to himself and he must try to find the right technique and medium which will give expression to that unique personal way of seeing. This will solve the question of which is the right type of medium and method to use. Much experimentation is essential and the way of trial and error is always the best.

13th Question: Does criticism by friends, even the most sympathetic of friends, help in one's creative work as a painter?

Answer: Yes—if you do not take the criticism to heart and also, what is more important, if you do not attempt to alter or modify your own view, because of anything said by anyone else. Perhaps encouragement is the only real help that your friends can give. But you must be stout-hearted and able to stand remarks passed by other people without letting them deflect or diminish your enthusiasm and perseverance. Remember that no one else sees in just the way you do and no one else can improve your view of things—it is only the constant practice of seeing and expressing in terms of your chosen medium, that gives added strength to your work.

14th Question: Is painting with a palette knife, almost exclusively, a justifiable technique of oil painting?

Answer: This, of course, is a very personal matter. I myself have consistently used the palette knife as a *main* tool for painting all types of pictures for very many years and found it exactly suited to my vision, and indeed a most excellent method. But many claim that it is not *real* painting and that brushes are the only tools for oil painting. It is only for certain kinds of strong impressionistic pictures that the thick paint and the palette knife strokes are exactly suited; therefore, on the whole, it is wise to use brushes for the most part and experiment with palette knife painting if you feel it will fit your type of vision of things better than the brush.

15th Question: How does one start painting a person's face or figure, and is such a thing possible without a study of anatomy?

Answer: If you are interested in faces and people above all other subjects, by all means start straight-away drawing and painting them. Try to see them in broad general terms of color patches, rather than in details of features, and also try to render the solidity of the head or figure by thinking of the head as a sphere and the body as a number of boxes and tubes. People, while the most interesting subjects of all to paint, are probably the most difficult, for they are always moving, and problems are created by the interaction between their feelings and thoughts and those of the artist.

I do not think it is necessary to have a knowledge of anatomy although a slight knowledge of the skull and the general bone formation is a help. But the great thing is to concentrate on the lines and shapes and colors that attract and interest you and put these down fearlessly, not considering or worrying about how accurate they are. Again, it is self-expression of your own viewpoint that matters all the time.

16th Question: Is it necessary to conform to set rules of composition, in order to compose a good picture?

Answer: No. Working out a composition on strictly conventional rules of composition is a dead proceeding. It is as well to start with the thing or point that interests you most and then work out to the edges of your given space, be it canvas or paper. You should have some idea of the general shapes that you wish to have in the picture and not just start off hoping that you will get things in their allotted places by a fluke. A small thumbnail sketch of the whole picture in very simplified form is a very good idea, to place the main masses and lines and the relations of dark shapes to light ones. This small preliminary sketch can be either in black and white (using a crayon or soft pencil) or in a few simple colors. Pastels are very good for this purpose.

17th Question: What part does a knowledge of the fundamental geometry of the sphere, cube, cone, and cylinder play in helping one to paint?

Answer: It does help to give a feeling of substance and depth to your work if you can, without straining your natural vision at all, see the third-dimensional aspect of things in nature. A tree in full leaf for instance, is not just flat, but goes round, and has depth as well as height and breadth. Conveying this impression is a matter of shading or making an alteration to the color according to which plane it is in, whether the front or the sides; and the sense of space and air behind things is conveyed by close observation of the contours and the lightening or darkening of the colors, according to what is behind each object.

18th Question: Is abstract painting justified—and all the other so-called "advanced" methods used by some artists today?

Answer: Yes, abstract painting, in which there are no actual objects reproduced, but just the simple essence of shapes, the square, the oblong, the circle, the triangle, and so forth, to make up the whole design of the picture, this abstract art is justified as reducing painting to its uttermost simplicity. It is only an exceptional artist who has this almost mathematical love of, and interest in, pure shape, and of course it is stupid to paint abstract pictures unless you feel deeply and intensely that only in this way can you express what you feel about things you see—you reduce them to their permanent logical conclusion of varying shapes and unify these shapes in your picture. All the other so-called "advanced-art" experiments are equally justified if they are sincere expressions. This is a wonderful time for experiment and for giving full vent to whatever ideas and visions you may have as you begin to see life in pictorial terms. These are, after all, but patches of color—"stains" if you like—on paper, wood, board, or canvas.

19th Question: How far does mounting, framing, and general presentation of pictures, affect their appeal?

Answer: If one wishes to send in the results of one's creative effort to selection committees (whose business it is to decide which pictures are exhibited, in all the multitude of exhibitions of pictures, open to outside exhibitors, up and down the country), then one has to pay careful attention to the right presentation of the work. That is, to see that it is suitably mounted and framed. This is always a tricky business and most artists find it irksome. It is probably best, if one can afford it, to go to an experienced framer and take his advice to begin with. A well-presented picture stands a hundred per cent better chance of being accepted for an exhibition than a shoddy, badly framed, or carelessly mounted picture of equal merit. You can look around second-hand shops and pick up useful frames sometimes. Then you have to paint the picture of the size to fit the frame, and bring the frame up to date by covering it with a coating of distemper, or alabastine, or similar substance, colored to the right color to suit the picture; not making the frame jump out away from the picture itself, nor too similar in color to the general color scheme of the picture, but of a tint that enhances the values and colors and improves the general appearance. The method of constant trial and error is here the only way.

20th Question: Is it possible to use the fragile medium of pastel successfully, to produce worthwhile pictures?

Answer: Yes. If pastel paintings are treated carefully and put under glass and backed up, so that air does not get to them, they keep perfectly for hundreds of years. The pastel medium is an excellent one to experiment with, for it needs probably less equipment than any other way of applying color, and you can get your color effects directly. Tinted boards, that do not bend or warp, are probably the best to use for working with pastels, and you can get almost any color by "cross hatching" one color over the top of another. Freshness and delicacy of handling are possible with this medium.

Index

Index

Index